KWIK·SEW'S
Sweatshirts Unlimited
by Kerstin Martensson

About the Author

KWIK•SEW'S SWEATSHIRTS UNLIMITED is the fourteenth book in a series of books on home sewing by Kerstin Martensson. Her previous best selling books have achieved world-wide success and popularity. The overwhelming acceptance of Kerstin Martensson's books can be attributed to their illustrated, easy-to-follow, step-by-step procedures. Over two million copies of her books have been sold thus far. Many of these are being used by schools and colleges throughout the western world as sewing textbooks.

Kerstin Martensson is the President of KWIK•SEW Pattern Co., Inc., and is internationally known as one of the foremost home economists. Kerstin was born in Gothenburg, Sweden and educated in both Sweden and England. She specialized in clothing construction, pattern design and fashion.

Kerstin has traveled extensively throughout the United States, Canada, Australia, England and the Scandinavian countries lecturing on her techniques to make sewing faster, easier and more fun.

Kerstin founded KWIK•SEW Pattern Co., Inc. in 1967 to make patterns for stretch fabrics as at that time none of the established pattern companies had patterns for this type of fabric. The company has grown into a world-wide operation with subsidiaries or offices in Australia, Canada and Europe. There are over eight hundred patterns in the KWIK•SEW pattern line and the line now includes patterns for all types of fabric.

Kerstin is encouraged by her customers' overwhelming response to her patterns and books, and she is dedicated to bringing the most up-to-date fashion and sewing techniques to the home sewer.

Introduction

KWIK•SEW'S SWEATSHIRTS UNLIMITED is a fun book. Everyone who sews would like the fun of creating a one-of-a-kind garment. Let your imagination run wild by the use of various inserts, colors, and fabrics on the same garment, this concept was unthinkable just a few years ago. Actually never has fashion been so much fun as right now.

The Master Pattern included in this book is for a sweatshirt in eight different sizes. Many people associate sweatshirts with a garment that should be worn when jogging and exercising, but this is no longer true. Sweatshirts have become a fashion garment, they can be for casual wear, sports and even dress-up occasions.

The sweatshirt is a loose fitting garment so you don't have to worry too much about the fit, which makes it a perfect gift for men, women and children. How about surprising a teenager with a sweatshirt using the school colors?

This book was written with the help of all the skilled staff in the Design and Art Departments of KWIK•SEW Pattern Company. Their combined talents have resulted in a book that is up-to-date, full of creative ideas and illustrations. Use this book and discover how much fun it is to create a one-of-a-kind garment.

Neckline finish: 7
Hem finish: 5
Sleeve finish: 1

Design change: H
Variation

Neckline finish: 1
Hem finish: 1
Sleeve finish: 1
Painting: Page 78

Neckline finish: 2
Hem finish: 1

Sleeve finish: 1
Patches and appliques

4

Contents

Neckline finish: 4
Hem finish: 1
Sleeve finish: 1

Design change: E
Applique

General Information

FABRICS

There are various types of fabric suitable for a sweatshirt. Use a knit fabric that doesn't have a lot of stretch. The most common are sweatshirt fleece, double knit, french terry and heavy single knit. Look through your fabric store and you will find novelty knits which are textured on the right side, these can also be used. These same fabrics may be used for the inserts. If you are using smaller pieces for the inserts, almost any type of woven fabric can be used.

For the cuffs, neckband and waistband, use ribbing which is available in a great variety of colors and sometimes even with stripes or designs.

When you are using different colors, we suggest you lay out the colors to try out the "effect" you wish to achieve and to be sure that the color combinations do not clash.

We suggest pre-washing all the fabric you will use in your garment, as some fabrics shrink and some colors will run which would ruin your sweatshirt.

If interfacing is required for stabilizing collars, etc., we recommend using a fusible interfacing.

PATTERNS

The Master Pattern included with this book is for a basic sweatshirt in eight sizes. All sizes are color coded to make it easier to follow the correct lines.

This is a unisex pattern. The smallest size has a chest measurement of 28" (71 cm) and will fit either a girl or boy size 10 or 12. The largest size has a chest measurement of 48" (122 cm) and will fit a man size Extra Large.

Also included in the Master Pattern are cuffs, waistband, pockets, and various designs of neckbands, plus overlays for the neckline. To use the pattern, select the neckline, sleeve and hem finish and refer to the correct section for complete instructions.

To make it easier for you to select the correct pattern pieces,
each one is numbered and identified, see the following chart.

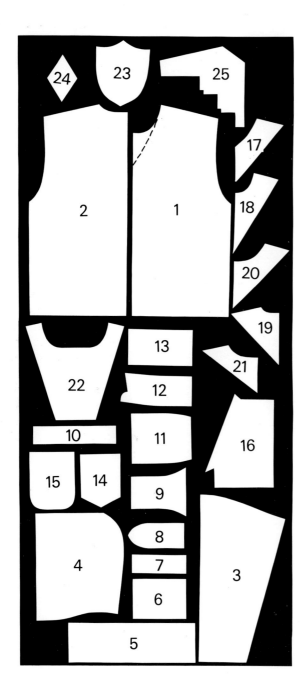

PATTERN PIECES

1. FRONT
2. BACK
3. SLEEVE
4. HOOD
5. WAISTBAND
6. CUFFS
7. NECKBAND
8. NECKBAND
9. NECKBAND
10. NECKBAND
11. COLLAR
12. COLLAR
13. COLLAR
14. POCKET
15. POCKET
16. POCKET
17. FRONT NECKLINE OVERLAY C
18. FRONT NECKLINE OVERLAY D
19. BACK NECKLINE OVERLAY D
20. FRONT NECKLINE OVERLAY E
21. BACK NECKLINE OVERLAY E
22. TAB FACING
23. CRESTS
24. DIAMOND PATCH
25. OVERLAY FOR OUTLINE STITCHING
    NUMBERS & LETTERS

A ¼" (6 mm) seam allowance is included on all pattern pieces. If you wish to change the seam allowance, this should be taken into consideration before you start cutting.

The Master Patterns are printed on both sides of the paper. You should trace the pattern so you can use the pattern over and over again. To trace the pattern, you can use tracing paper; however, it is easier if you use a tracing cloth which is composed of pressed fibers. The cloth is durable and will not tear, and it is transparent for easy tracing.

To offer you an unlimited variety of styles, we have divided the book into sections: Neckline finishes, Hem and Sleeve finishes, Pockets, Design Changes and Decorative finishes. For example, in the section for the neckline finishes, each neck variation is numbered. The color photos throughout the book will indicate which finish is used for the neckline, hem and sleeves, and which design change was used. To create your own design, you can take an idea from one photo and combine it with an idea from another. This is where you become creative and the fun begins.

You may also wish to coordinate your sweatshirt with a skirt, pants or shorts. Although this book contains a Master Pattern for a Shirt only, we suggest you check your local fabric store to choose the KWIK•SEW Pattern of your choice to coordinate an outfit.

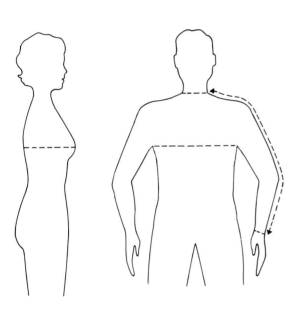

HOW TO CHOOSE SIZE

It is very important to choose the correct size pattern, this should be determined by the chest or bust measurement. Measure the body around the largest part of the bust or chest. Compare your measurement to the chest measurement given on the chart and choose the size closest to your measurement.

If your measurements fall between the measurements on this chart, use your own judgment to determine if you would prefer to have a tighter or looser fit. Please note on the chart that the finished width of the sweatshirt is larger than the body measurement, this is to give a loose fit.

Chest Size	28	30	33	36	39	42	45	48	
Chest or Bust Body Measurement	28 (71)	30 (76)	33 (84)	36 (91)	39 (99)	42 (107)	45 (114)	48 (122)	" (cm)
Finished Width of Shirt at Chest & Hip	35 (89)	38 (96)	41 (104)	44 (112)	46½ (118)	50 (127)	53 (134)	56 (142)	" (cm)
Finished Length at Center Back Including a 2½" (6.5 cm) Wide Waistband	22¼ (56)	23¾ (60)	25 (63)	26 (66)	27 (68)	28 (71)	29 (74)	30 (77)	" (cm)
Finished Length of Shoulder & Sleeve Including a 2½" (6.5 cm) Wide Cuff	24½ (62)	26 (66)	27½ (70)	28¾ (73)	30 (76)	31¼ (79)	32½ (83)	34 (86)	" (cm)

ADJUSTING LENGTH

It is also important to obtain the correct sleeve and body length. For the sleeves, measure the distance from the base of the neck, over the shoulder, down to the wrist. For the length of the sweatshirt, measure the back from the top of the neck bone down to the desired length. Compare your measurements to the measurements given on the chart on Page 9. The finished length given includes a 2½" (6.5 cm) waistband and a 2½" (6.5 cm) cuff. If you are making a sweatshirt without waistband and cuffs, be sure to add length to the front, back and sleeves.

Shorten

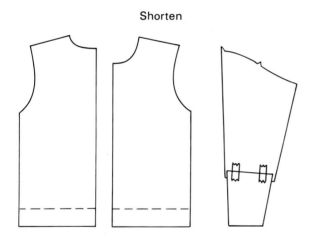

To shorten or lengthen the body of the shirt, add or deduct the same amount on the front and back at the bottom edge. To shorten or lengthen the sleeves, cut the pattern apart on the shorten and lengthen line given. Overlap the pattern pieces to shorten and spread the pattern apart to lengthen.

Lengthen

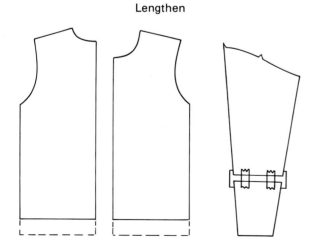

CUTTING

When cutting any type of fabric, it is very important to use a pair of sharp scissors to obtain a clean cut. Dull scissors have a tendency to chew the fabric rather than cut it. If they should become dull, get them sharpened as soon as possible.

When you have cut out the pattern pieces, it is a good idea to mark each piece so that you do not mix them up. We recommend using transparent tape; place a small piece on the wrong side of the fabric, marking the side seams, back, etc. This tape has a dull finish which you can write on. Always use a pencil, as a ballpoint pen could spot the fabric and ink is difficult to wash out.

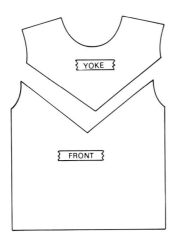

Fabric for sweatshirts usually comes approximately 60" (152 cm) wide. Because the fabric often is doubled when put on a bolt, you sometimes get a crease at the fold. Before cutting, try to press out this crease. If you are unable to press out the crease, refold the fabric so that the crease is not in a conspicuous place.

When cutting out the pattern pieces always be sure to follow the arrows so that the grain and stretch of the fabric is in the right direction.

SEWING

When making a sweatshirt use either cotton or synthetic thread and use a 12/80 ball point sewing machine needle. You can use any type of conventional sewing machine or a serger (overlock) machine.

STANDARD SEWING MACHINE

When sewing the sweatshirt, use either a medium length straight stitch or a narrow zig-zag stitch. Overcast the raw edges with a zig-zag stitch or a three-step zig-zag stitch. If you do not have a zig-zag stitch on your machine, sew the seam allowances together close to the raw edges.

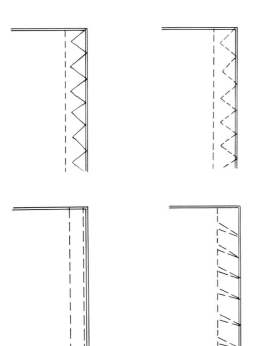

When you are working with a ¼" (6 mm) seam allowance and you have a reverse cycle machine, you can use an overlock stitch. This stitch sews the seam and overcasts in one operation.

SERGER (OVERLOCK) MACHINE

This type of sewing machine gives a very professional look. Serger (overlock) machines sew, overcast and trim the excess seam allowance in one step. When using a serger (overlock) machine, be sure that you are using the correct seam allowance so that the garment will fit properly. Try the seam on a scrap piece of fabric and mark the location for the edge of the fabric. Guide the edge of the fabric along this line.

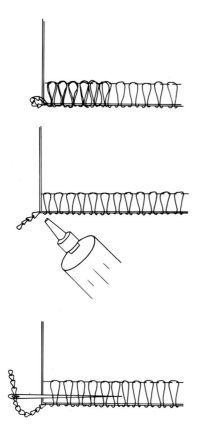

If necessary to lock the seams at the ends, use any of the following methods:

Sew a chain, then turn the fabric and sew for about 1" (2.5 cm).

Use "Fray Check"® which glues the threads together.

Sew a chain and insert the chain through the seam with a large needle or crochet hook.

It is very important to press the seams as you sew them. After sewing the seams, always press them flat first. When you are making a seam, using a ¼" (6 mm) seam allowance, press the seam allowances toward one side.

Topstitching is very attractive on a sweatshirt. You can use a single or double needle, or if you have an elastic straight stitch, it will give you a heavier seam; however, be sure to use a longer than medium stitch length.

Topstitching ¼" (6 mm) or wider from seam will require a ⅝" (1.5 cm) seam allowance. Be sure to add ⅜" (1 cm) when cutting. The ⅝" (1.5 cm) seam allowances can be pressed open and topstitched on each side of the seam, or it can be pressed to one side and topstitched close to the seam and again ¼" (6 mm) from the first topstitching.

Double Needle

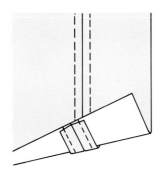
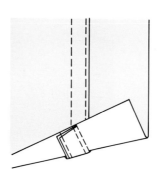
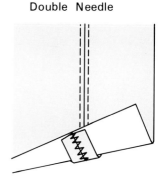

Basic Sweatshirt

The basic instructions for a sweatshirt are the same for all types of sweatshirts shown throughout the book. All variations will be explained when appropriate. Basic instructions include Neckline Finish 1 — crew neck, Hem Finish 1 — waistband, and Sleeve Finish 1 — cuffs.

For the basic sweatshirt, use pattern pieces:
1. Front
2. Back
3. Sleeve
5. Waistband
6. Cuffs
7. Neckband

Trace the pattern pieces. Trace the line for neckline A on both the front and the back pattern pieces. If you need to shorten or lengthen the sweatshirt, do this before you cut out the fabric.

Neckline finish: 1
Hem finish: 1

Sleeve finish: 1
Applique

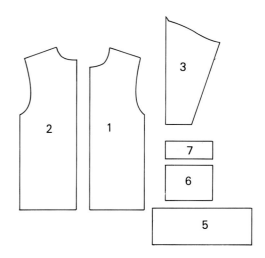

Neckline finish: 3
Hem finish: 1
Sleeve finish: 1

Design change: J
Pocket: 2

YARDAGE REQUIREMENT

Yardage requirements are for the basic shirt using 60" (152 cm) wide fabric. If using a variation, use the yardage requirement only as a guide.

Size	28	30	33	36	
	1⅛ (1.05)	1¼ (1.15)	1¼ (1.15)	1⅜ (1.30)	yd (m)

Size	39	42	45	48	
	1⅜ (1.30)	1½ (1.40)	1½ (1.40)	1⅝ (1.50)	yd (m)

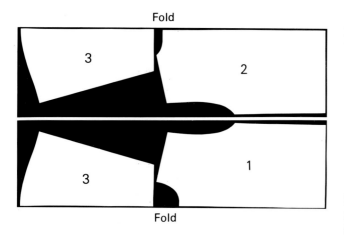

Fold

Fold the fabric double with the right sides together. Place pattern pieces 1, 2 and 3 on the fabric, see layout. Layout is given for the basic shirt only, if using any variations, use the layout only as a guide. Cut out the pattern pieces.

For the neckband, waistband, and cuffs, you should use ribbing, make sure to follow arrows for grain and stretch of fabric. Cut out pattern pieces 5, 6 and 7 from the ribbing.

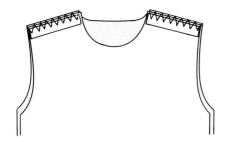

SEWING BASIC SHIRT

SHOULDERS

To eliminate stretching of the shoulder seams, you can sew a non-stretch seam binding to the shoulder seams. Cut a piece of seam binding the length of the shoulder; use the pattern piece to measure, or you can use a piece of fusible interfacing ½" (1.3 cm) wide and the length of the shoulder.

Pin the front to the back, right sides together. Place the stabilizing strip at the front shoulder and sew the shoulder seam through all layers. Press the shoulder seam toward the back.

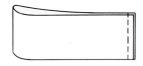

NECKLINE FINISH 1
CREWNECK

Sew the ends of the neckband together to form a circle by folding the band right side to right side. Sew the seam, using a straight stitch and press the seam open.

Fold and pin the neckband double, wrong sides and raw edges together. Divide the neckband and the neckline into fourths with pins. At the neckline, a pin should be at the center back and the center front.

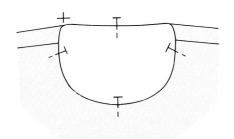

Pin the neckband to the right side of the neckline with the raw edges together. Match the seam to the center back and pin in place, matching the remaining pins.

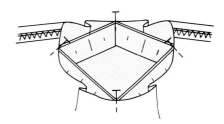

Sew the neckband to the neckline, stretching the neckband between the pins so that it will fit the neckline. The easiest way to do this is to always have the smallest piece on top. In this case, the neckline is underneath and the neckband is on top.

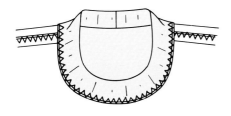

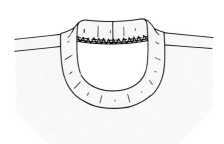

To obtain a professional looking neckline, it is very important to press the neckline after you have sewn on the neckband. Place the neckline over a pressing ham and steam press the neckline into shape. Press the seam toward the shirt.

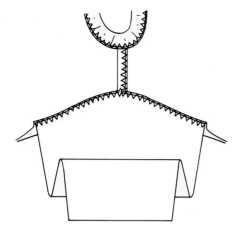

SLEEVES AND SIDE SEAMS

Sew the sleeves in place before you sew the side seams and the sleeve seams. Match center notch of the sleeve to the shoulder seam and the underarm edges.

Starting at the bottom of the shirt sew the side seam and the sleeve seam in one continuous step.

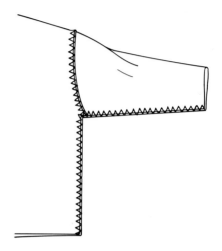

HEM FINISH 1
RIBBING WAISTBAND

Sew the side seams of the waistband together, right side to right side to form a circle. Press the seams open.

Fold the waistband double lengthwise with the wrong side and raw edges together. Divide the waistband and the bottom edge into fourths with pins.

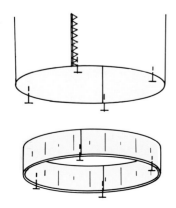

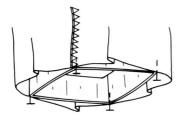

Pin the waistband to the bottom edge with the right sides and the raw edges together. Place the seams on the waistband at the side seams and match the remaining pins. Sew on the waistband, stretching it to fit the bottom edge of the sweatshirt.

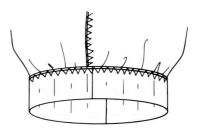

SLEEVE FINISH 1
RIBBING CUFFS

Sew the sleeve seams of the cuffs together to form circles. Press seam open. Fold each cuff lengthwise, wrong sides together. Divide the cuffs and the sleeve openings in half with pins.

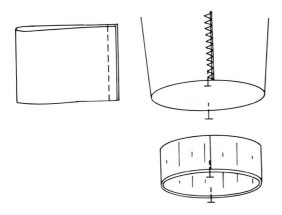

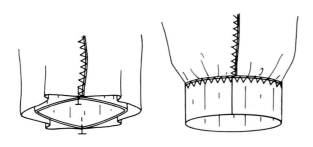

Match the seam on the cuff to the seam on the sleeve. Pin the cuff to the sleeve opening, right sides and raw edges together, matching the pins. Sew on the cuffs, stretching the cuffs to fit the sleeve openings.

Neckline Finishes

When you are making a sweatshirt, you can have a wide variety of neckline finishes. This is also a perfect opportunity to play with colors. For example, the color for the neckband and cuffs can be the same as the skirt or pants you plan to wear with the shirt. If you plan to use contrast color inserts, the neckband and cuffs would look very attractive in the same color as the inserts. Perhaps you may like to use a striped collar with matching cuffs and waistband. Color variations are endless. This is where you can apply your imagination.

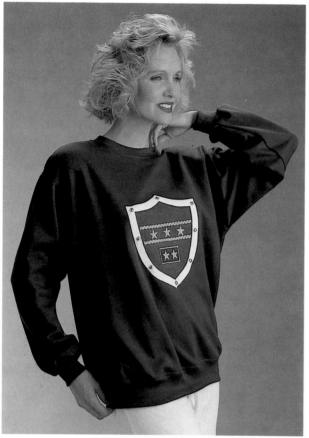

Neckline finish: 1
Hem finish: 1

Sleeve finish: 1
Crests: Page 68

It is important to use the correct cutting line for the front and the back neckline finish you have selected. Neckline A and B are included on the front pattern piece, neckline A, B and C are included on the back pattern piece. For the remaining necklines, use the neckline overlays.

To use the overlay for a neckline, trace the overlay and place it on the front, matching the center front and shoulder lines. Repeat for the back using the overlay for the back. Now trace the front and back pattern pieces using the neckline of the overlay.

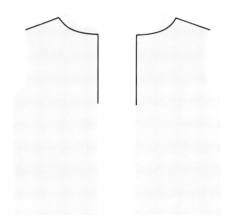

The Basic sweatshirt includes instructions for the basic crew neckband Neckline Finish 1 on Page 15. These same sewing instructions are used for almost all the neckbands. Variations are described when necessary.

Neckline finish: 2
Sleeve finish: 1

Sleeve finish: 1
Design change: D

NECKLINE FINISH 2
TURTLENECK & MOCK TURTLENECK

A turtleneck has a wide band which is turned over. A mock turtleneck has a wide band which is not turned over.

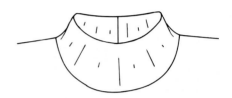

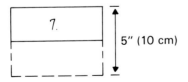

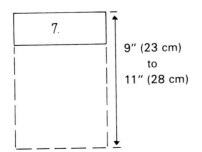

When you cut out the front and back, use cutting line A for the neckline. Use Master Pattern piece 7 for neckband. For a mock turtleneck band, increase the width of pattern piece 7 so it is approximately 5" (10 cm) wide. For a turtleneck band, increase the width to be between 9" (23 cm) to 11" (28 cm), cut neckbands from ribbing.

Sew as Neckline Finish 1 on Page 15.

Neckline finish: 2
Lettuce edging
Hem finish: 7

Sleeve finish: 1
Decorative yoke: Page 76

LETTUCE EDGING

The outside edge of any width neckband, can be finished with lettuce edging. Set the machine to a wider than medium zig-zag width and a very short stitch length. Zig-zag over the outer edge of the neckband, stretching the neckband as much as possible while sewing.

A serger (overlock) machine may be used; but be careful not to cut the edge while sewing.

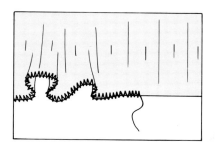

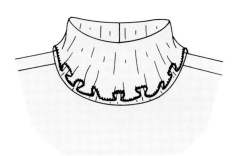

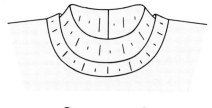

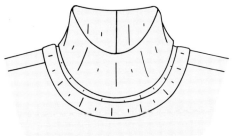

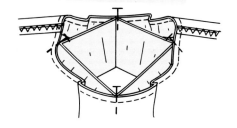

NECKLINE FINISH 3
DOUBLE NECKBAND

A double neckband is sometimes used to give the impression that there is another shirt underneath the sweatshirt. To emphasize this, it looks best if you use two different colors.

Use Master Pattern piece 7. Cut one band the same size as the pattern piece. Cut another band 1" (2.5 cm) wider or the same width as for a turtleneck. See Page 19.

Baste the narrow neckband to the neckline, following Neckline Finish 1 on page 15. Pin the wider neckband over the narrow band and sew through all layers, stretching the bands to fit the neckline.

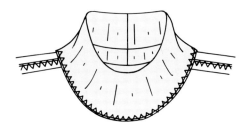

Neckline finish: 4
Hem finish: 1
Sleeve finish: 1

Design change: I
Purchased label

NECKLINE FINISH 4
NECKBAND AND COLLAR

A neckband and collar combination makes an attractive neckline. Use Master Pattern piece 7 for the neckband. Baste the neckband to the neckline, following Neckline Finish 1 on Page 15.

The collar can be cut from ribbing or use a purchased finished ribbed collar.

Use Master Pattern piece 11 to cut the collar from ribbing. Fold the collar double lengthwise, right side to right side and sew the ends of the collar. Turn the collar right side out. Sew the ends of the collar together with a few hand stitches on the seam allowance.

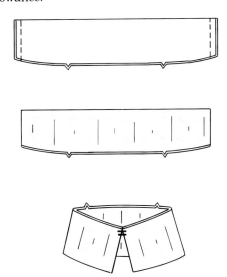

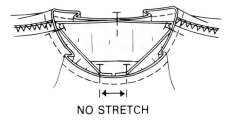

NO STRETCH

Pin the collar to the right side of the neckline, over the neckband with the raw edges together and the ends of the collar at the center front. Match the notches to the shoulder seams and match the center backs. When you pin the collar, do not stretch the collar for 1" (2.5 cm) on each side of the center front. Sew through all layers, stretching the collar and neckband to fit the opening.

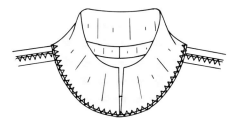

If you are using a finished ribbed collar, fold the collar double lengthwise, and compare the width and the length to pattern piece 11. Place the finished edge of the collar on the fold line of the pattern and trim the neckline, following the pattern piece.

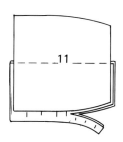

11

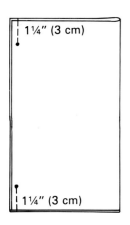

Neckline finish: 5
Hem finish: 6

Sleeve finish: 6
Design change: I

NECKLINE FINISH 5
SPLIT RIBBING COLLAR

A collar made from ribbing can be folded to look like a regular collar or it can stand up. This type of collar is often referred to as a split mock or turtleneck.

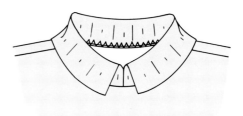

Use Master Pattern piece 7. For a stand up collar, cut the band approximately 5" (13 cm) wide. For a fold over collar, cut the band approximately 7½" (19 cm) wide.

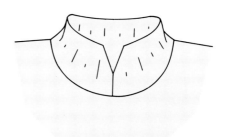

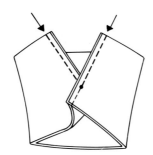

Fold the collar in half, right side to right side. Sew 1¼" (3 cm) on either side as illustrated. Fold the collar double, right side to right side. Using a straight stitch, sew from the folded edges and stop at the previous stitches. Press the seam open. Turn the collar right side out. Place the seam of the collar at the center front and sew on the collar.

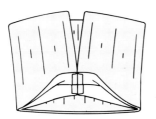

Adding a few tiny buttons to center front gives the shirt a dressier look.

Neckline finish: 6
Hem finish: 5

Sleeve finish: 1
Pocket with patch: 1

NECKLINE FINISH 6
CROSS-OVER CREW NECKBAND

Use Master Pattern piece 8. You may adjust the width of this neckband to be as wide or narrow as you choose.

To adjust the width, cut the pattern piece at the fold line and overlap or spread to the width desired.

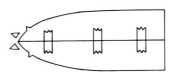 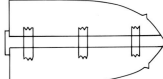

Fold the neckband double lengthwise, wrong side to wrong side. Overlap the ends of the neckband, matching the notches. Pin in place. When you sew on the neckband, match notches to the center front of the sweatshirt.

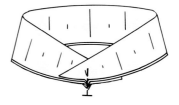

NECKLINE FINISH 7
V-MOCK TURTLENECK

A V-mock turtleneck can be made with or without a slit. Use neckline overlay Master Pattern piece 17 for the front neckline. Cut out the pattern using neckline C on the front and on the back. Use Master Pattern piece 9 for the neckband and cut from ribbing.

On front, staystitch the point of the V, using a straight stitch, 1" (2.5 cm) on each side and ¼" (6 mm) in from the raw edges. Make a clip at the point of the V to the stitches.

Neckline finish: 7
Hem finish: 1
Sleeve finish: 1

Fold the band double, right side to right side. Sew the center back seam. Press the seam open.

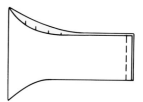

Fold the band double lengthwise, wrong side to wrong side. Divide the neckband and the neckline into fourths, using pins.

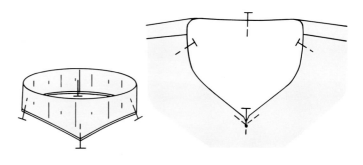

Pin the neckband to the neckline, right side to right side. Match the point of the neckband to the center front. Sew on the neckband. When you come to the point of the V, lower the needle into the fabric, pivot, and sew the other side.

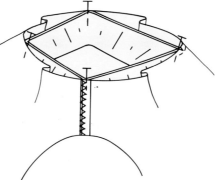

For a V-mock turtleneck with a slit, use Master Pattern piece 9. When cutting out the neckband, place the center back on the fold and place the seam at the center front.

To make the slit in the neckband, refer to Neckline Finish 5 on Page 22.

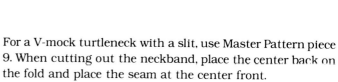

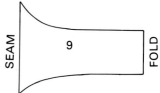

Neckline finish: 8
Hem finish: 8

Sleeve finish: 1
Patch

NECKLINE FINISH 8
NECKBAND WITH INSERT

As a variation of a regular neckband, you can make an insert using the same fabric as the sweatshirt. Cut out sweatshirt, using neckline A on the front and the back. Use Master Pattern piece 7 for the neckband, shorten the pattern 1" (2.5 cm) and cut from ribbing. Cut a strip of self fabric 3" (7.5 cm) long and the same width as the neckband.

1" (2.5 cm)

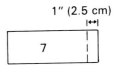

Sew this strip to the ends of the neckband, right sides together. Press the seams open. Fold the neckband double lengthwise, wrong sides together. Place the fabric insert at the center front and sew the neckband to the neckline. If you wish, you can topstitch the insert for a special effect.

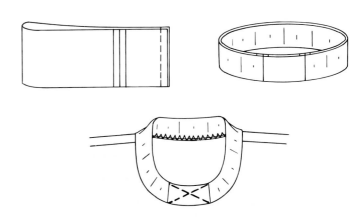

NECKLINE FINISH 9
RIBBING BINDING

Use Master Pattern piece 7 for the binding. Add 1" (2.5 cm) to the length of the pattern piece and ⅜" (1 cm) to the width. Cut the binding from ribbing.

1" (2.5 cm)

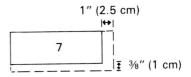

⅜" (1 cm)

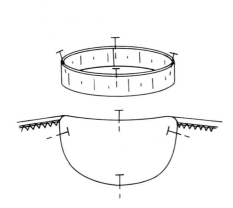

Sew neckline binding right sides together, using a straight stitch and press seam open. Fold binding double lengthwise, wrong sides and raw edges together. Divide binding and neckline into fourths with pins.

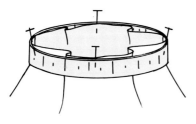

Pin the binding to the wrong side of the neckline with the raw edges together, matching pins and seam to center back. Sew on the binding, stretching it to fit the neckline.

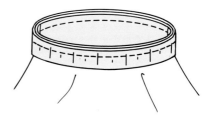

Press the seam allowance toward the garment. Sew through the seam allowance and the fabric close to the seam. Trim the seam allowance close to the stitches.

Fold the binding at the seam to the right side, over the seam allowance, and pin in place. Topstitch close to the edge of the binding. A very attractive finish is obtained by using a double needle for the topstitching.

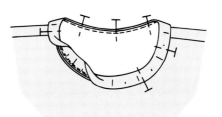

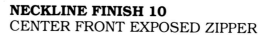

NECKLINE FINISH 10
CENTER FRONT EXPOSED ZIPPER

An exposed zipper is not only attractive, it is also practical when you do not want to have your hair in disarray.

Use Master Pattern piece 13 for the collar and neckline overlay Master Pattern pieces 18 and 19. Cut out the front and the back using neckline D. You can use any length zipper, but remember you have to allow 2¼" (5.5 cm) extra for the collar.

Mark the center front with basting stitches or use a water soluable pen. Cut a partial slit at center front approximately 3" (7.5 cm) down from the neckline.

Neckline finish: 10
Hem finish: 2
Sleeve finish: 1

Design change: Basic
Patches

Press the collar double lengthwise, wrong side to wrong side. Pin one edge of the collar, to the neckline, right side to right side. Match the center back, dots to shoulder seams and the ends of the collar to the center front. Sew on the collar.

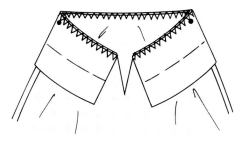

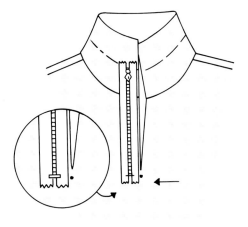

To obtain the correct length of the zipper slit, place the zipper with the pull at the folding line on collar and mark the length at the zipper stop. Continue cutting the slit, stopping ¼" (6 mm) from the mark.

Place the bottom edge of the zipper at the bottom of the slit, be sure to place the right side of the zipper to the right side of the front. The bottom of the zipper teeth should be at the mark. The zipper is in the opposite direction from the cut opening. Hold the zipper in place with transparent tape.

Sew a few stitches the width of the zipper teeth at the bottom to secure the zipper. Remove the tape. Clip the seam allowance close to the stitches as illustrated.

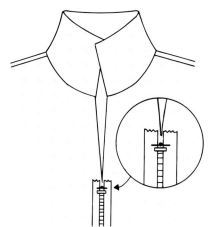

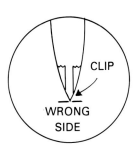

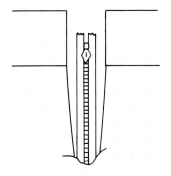

Flip the zipper into the correct position.

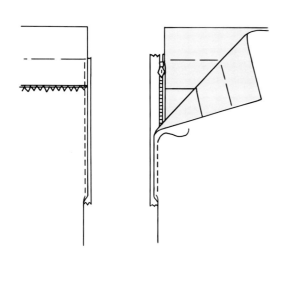

Fold one side of the fabric over the zipper, right side to right side, and baste as close as possible to the zipper teeth. The seam allowance will be very narrow. Follow the same procedure for the other side. Sew each side of the zipper.

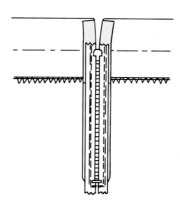

At the top, fold down the zipper tape toward the center front and pin. Fold the extending collar to the right side over the zipper. Sew the width of the collar on the same stitching line as for inserting the zipper.

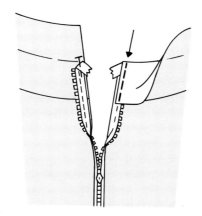

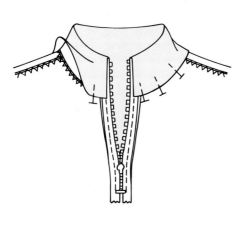

Turn the collar right side out. Press the neckline seam allowance toward the collar. On the inside, pin the free edge of the collar over the seam. On the right side, secure the collar by sewing as close as possible to the neckline seam.

Topstitch around the zipper ¼" (6 mm) from the edge.

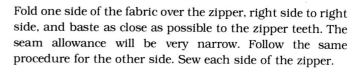

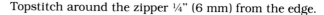

NECKLINE FINISH 11
BOAT NECKLINE WITH FACING

Use overlay Master Pattern pieces 20 and 21. Cut out the back and front using neckline E. You need a facing for the neckline on the back and the front. To make facing, measure from the outer edge of the neckline, 1½" (4 cm) and make a line following the curve of the neckline. Trace and cut out the facing pieces. Facing can be made from the same fabric as the sweatshirt or a contrasting woven fabric can be used.

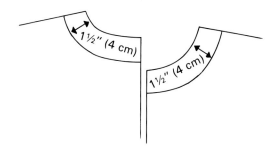

Stabilize the facings on the wrong side, using fusible interfacing. Place the facings, right side to right side, and sew the shoulder seams.

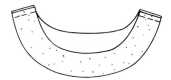

Pin the facing to the neckline, right side to right side, matching the center back, center front and shoulder seams. Sew in place and clip seam allowance.

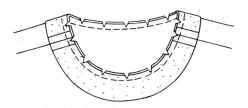

Press the seam allowance toward the facing and understitch. Fold the facing to the inside and press. Topstitch around the neckline 1" (2.5 cm) from the edge.

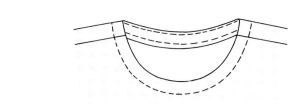

Neckline finish: 11
Hem finish: 2

Sleeve finish: 10
Patch

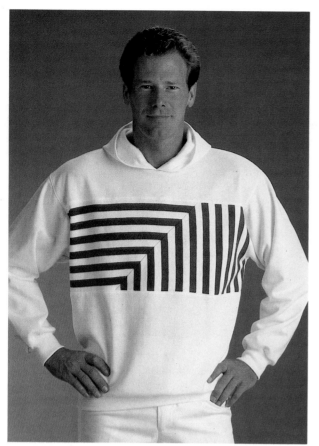

Neckline finish: 12
Hem finish: 1

Sleeve finish: 1
Design change: G

NECKLINE FINISH 12
HOOD

A hood is fashionable, practical and easy to make. Use Master Pattern piece 4 for the hood and neckline A for the front and back.

Overcast the raw edges on the front facing of hood. Press the facing to the wrong side on the folding line. Sew down the facing close to the raw edges. Place the hood, double, right side to right side, and sew the center back seam.

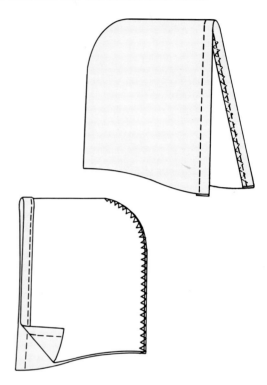

At center front, at the bottom of the hood, sew a few stitches to keep the front of the hood together. Pin the hood to the neckline, right side to right side, matching the center front, center back, and the dots to the shoulder seams. Sew the hood in place. Press the seam allowance toward the neckline and topstitch close to the seam.

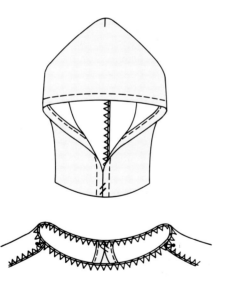

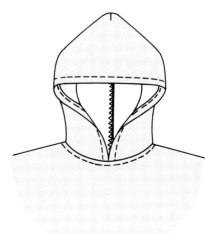

Neckline finish: 13
Hem finish: 1

Sleeve finish: 1
Pocket: 7

NECKLINE FINISH 13
PLACKET WITH COLLAR

A sweatshirt with a placket and collar gives a more dressy look. This is especially true if a woven fabric is used for the collar and the placket.

The pattern and instructions are given for a placket which overlaps left over right, this is for men and boys. If you want to change to right over left for women and girls, change the placket and the marking for the slit to the opposite side and reverse all instructions for the left and the right sides.

Use Master Pattern piece 12 Collar and 22 Tab Facing. Trace Neckline Overlays 18 and 19. Cut out the front and back pattern pieces following neckline D. Fuse interfacing to the wrong side of the tab facing. Transfer the marking for the slit to the interfaced side of the tab facing and to the right front.

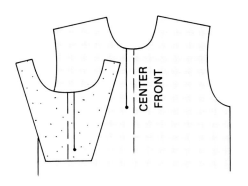

Pin the tab facing to the front, right side to right side, matching the markings for the slit. Using a straight stitch, sew ⅛" (3 mm) from the marking on each side. At the bottom of the slit sew to a point. Cut the slit down to the point.

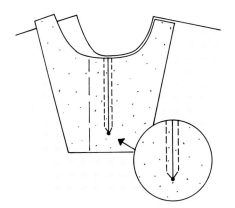

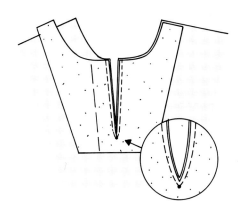

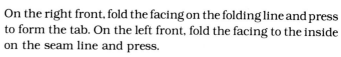

On the right front, fold the facing on the folding line and press to form the tab. On the left front, fold the facing to the inside on the seam line and press.

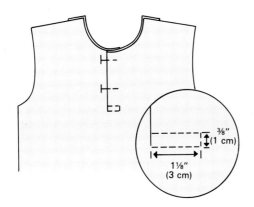

⅜"
(1 cm)

1⅛"
(3 cm)

Overlap the left front over the right front and pin through all layers. At the bottom of the slit, sew a ⅜" (1 cm) by 1⅛" (3 cm) rectangle through all layers of fabric.

Fuse interfacing to the wrong side of one collar. Pin the collars, right side to right side and sew the outside edges, leaving the neckline open. Trim the corners and clip the curved seam allowances.

Turn collar right side out. Press the collar, rolling the seam toward the under collar side, this will prevent the seam from showing from the right side. If you wish, you can topstitch the collar close to the edges.

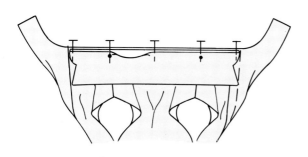

Pin the collar to the right side of the neckline, matching the center back, dots to the shoulder seams, and the ends of the collar to the edges of the front (on Left Front at seam for facing, on Right Front at folding line).

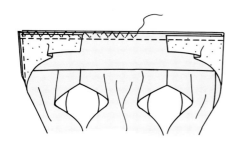

Fold the facing over the collar to the right side. Sew the collar through all layers.

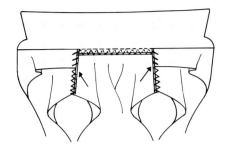

Turn the facing to the inside and press. Attach ends of facings to shoulder seams.

Make one or two vertical buttonholes on the left front and one horizontal buttonhole on the collar stand. Sew on buttons to match the buttonholes.

This neckline finish is also nice if you use a ribbing collar or a finished ribbed collar. Use Master Pattern piece 11. Follow instructions on Page 21.

When sewing on the collar, place the ends of the collar at the center front. On right front, center front is in the middle of the tab, on left front ¾" (2 cm) from edge of the front.

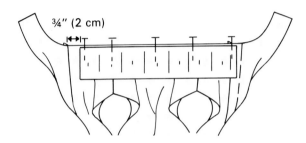

NECKLINE FINISH 14
V-NECK

When cutting out the sweatshirt, use cutting line B for both the front and the back neckline. Use Master Pattern piece 10 for the neckband. Cut the neckband from ribbing.

Staystitch the point of the V, using a straight stitch, ¼" (6 mm) from the raw edges. Make a clip at the point of the V to the stitches. Sew the shoulder seams.

Neckline finish: 14
Hem finish: 1

Sleeve finish: 1
Pockets: 3

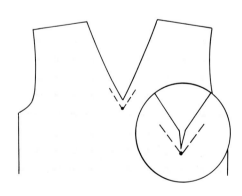

Fold the neckband double, right side to right side. Sew the center back seam and press it open. Fold the band double, lengthwise, wrong side to wrong side.

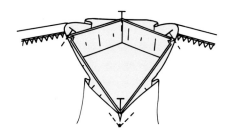

Pin the neckband to the neckline, right side to right side, matching the center front, the center back, and the notches to the shoulder seams.

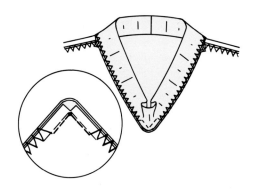

Sew on the neckband, stretching the neckband to fit the opening. When you come to the point of the V, lower the needle into the fabric, pivot and sew up the other side.

Fold the front and the band, right sides together, along the center front. Sew the center front seam of the neckband from the outside edge of the band to the seam in line with the center front fold.

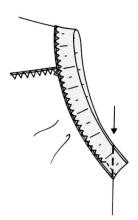

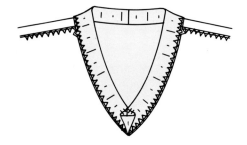

On the inside, open the seam and attach with a few stitches by hand.

NECKLINE FINISH 15
YOKE WITH FRONT BUTTONS

A shirt with a front opening and a neckband is easy to make when you have a front yoke. Trace front and back following Neckline A. On front armhole, divide in half between notch and the bottom of the armhole. Draw a line for the yoke. Cut pattern apart and add ⅝" (1.5 cm) seam allowance to yoke and front.

On the yoke, add 1⅝" (4 cm) to the center front. Mark the center front.

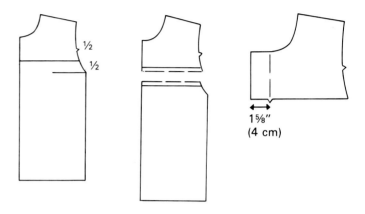

Cut two strips of fusible interfacing 1" (2.5 cm) wide and the distance from the neckline to the yoke seam. Fuse the interfacing to the wrong sides of the front edges. Fold a 1" (2.5 cm) facing to the wrong side and press.

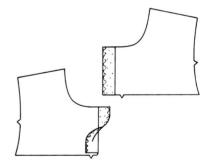

Use Master Pattern piece 8 for the neckband and cut from ribbing. Sew the shoulder seams. Fold the neckband double lengthwise, wrong side to wrong side with the raw edges together. Pin the neckband to the neckline, right side to right side and raw edges together, matching the center back and with the ends of the neckband at the folding lines of the yoke.

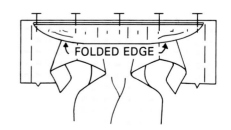

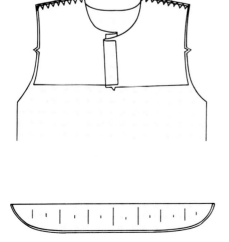

Neckline finish: 15　　　Sleeve finish: 1
Hem finish: 1　　　　　Design change: Basic

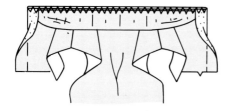

Fold the front facings on the folding lines to the right side over the neckband. Sew the neckband to the neckline through all layers, stretching the neckband to fit the neckline.

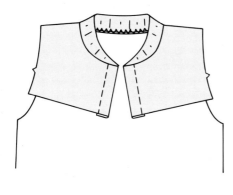

Turn the facing to the wrong side. Topstitch close to edge of facing. Overlap the left yoke over the right, matching the center front. Sew across to keep it in place.

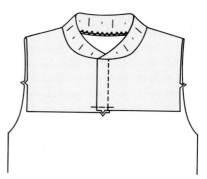

Sew the front yoke to the front. Make buttonholes and sew on the buttons, or you may use snaps.

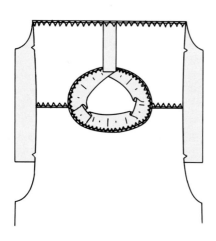

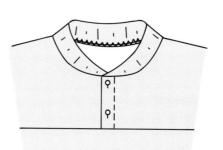

Hem & Sleeve Finishes

Your basic shirt has a ribbing waistband and cuffs, Hem and sleeve finish 1 on Pages 16 and 17. There are additional ways to finish the hem and sleeves, such as, using elastic, slits, drawstring, etc.

Whatever method is used, be sure to get the correct length on both the shirt and the sleeves. Compare your measurements with the pattern and follow the instructions for each finish. Remember your basic shirt allows for a 2½" (6.5 cm) wide waistband and cuffs. If you are making a hemline finish without the waistband and cuffs, you may need to add length to the bottom edge of the shirt and sleeves.

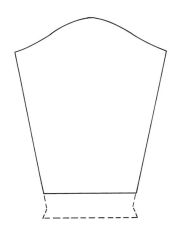

HEM FINISH 2
FINISHED WITH HEMS

When you cut out the front and back pattern pieces, check for the correct finished length. Refer to Page 9. Add 1"-2" (2.5 cm - 5 cm) for the hem. For the sleeves, also check length and add 1"-2" (2.5 cm - 5 cm) for the hem. To be able to fold up the hem at the bottom edge of the sleeves without puckering, it has to be the same width as the sleeve. Add to the sides of the hem, see illustration. Overcast the bottom edges of the sleeves and the shirt. Fold the hem to the wrong side and press. Sew the hem with a straight stitch close to the overcasted edge or sew the hem on the right side using a double needle.

HEM FINISH 3
BAND FROM CONTRASTING FABRIC

Adding a band from woven fabric to the bottom of the sweatshirt or to the sleeves, gives a different look. Check for correct finished length. Refer to Page 9.

You can use any width of band; however, we suggest that you cut the band 6½" (16.5 cm) wide, this makes the finished band 3" (7.5 cm) wide. The length should be the same as the bottom edge, plus seam allowances. Sew the ends of the band together, right side to right side, to form a circle.

Press the band double lengthwise, wrong side to wrong side with the raw edges together. Pin the band to the right side of the bottom edge of the shirt, placing the seams of the band at side seams. Sew on the band.

Neckline finish: 11
Hem finish: 3

Sleeve finish: 10
Pocket: 3

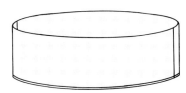
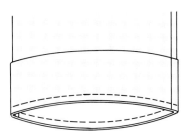

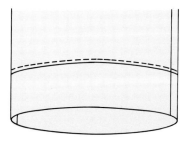

Press the seam allowance toward the shirt and topstitch close to the seam.

For another effect, add piping in the seam.

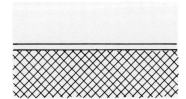

HEM FINISH 4
RIBBING WITH DRAWSTRING

Check for correct finished length. Refer to Page 9. Use Master Pattern piece 5 for the waistband. Add 2" (5 cm) to the length of the pattern piece. Cut waistband from ribbing.

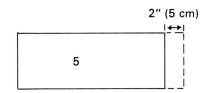

Fold one waistband in half and mark the center front. Mark the position for two vertical buttonholes, ½" (1.3 cm) from the center front and 2" (5 cm) from the edge. Place a piece of interfacing on the wrong side, under the position of the buttonholes. Make the buttonholes.

CENTER
FRONT

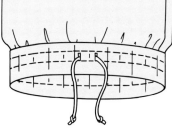

2" (5 cm)

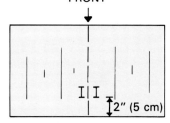

Sew the side seams. Fold the waistband double lengthwise, wrong side to wrong side. In the middle of the band, sew a ½" (1.3 cm) casing for the drawstring. Sew the waistband to the bottom edge of the sweatshirt. Make sure that the buttonholes are on the front and the outside. Insert a drawstring through the buttonholes.

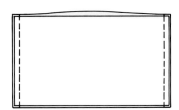

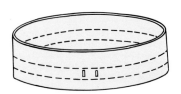

Neckline finish: 13
Hem finish: 5
Sleeve finish: 1

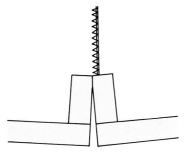

HEM FINISH 5
SIDE HEMLINE SLITS

The slits can be as long as you wish. The instructions are for a 3" (7.5 cm) slit. Check for the correct finished length of the shirt. Refer to Page 9. Add 1½" (4 cm) for the hem. On the side seam of the back and the front pattern pieces, add a 1¼" (3 cm) wide and 4¾" (8 cm) long facing for the slit.

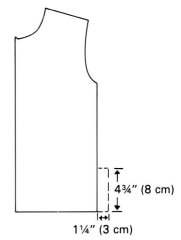

4¾" (8 cm)

1¼" (3 cm)

Sew the sweatshirt, following the basic instructions to the point of sewing the side seams.

Start sewing the side seam 4½" (7.5 cm) from the bottom edge and sew to the bottom edge of the sleeve.

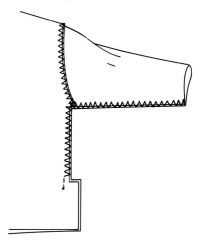

To finish the bottom of the slit, fold a 1½" (4 cm) hem to the right side and sew a seam 1½" (4 cm) from the edge. Trim the hem on the facing. Turn the corners inside out and press. Sew close to the edges of the facing and the hem.

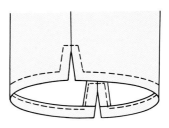

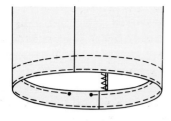

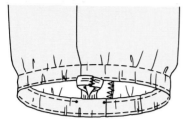

HEM FINISH 6
ELASTIC IN CASING AT BOTTOM EDGE

When cutting out the back and front pattern, check for correct length and add 1½" (4 cm) for the casing, this is for 1" (2.5 cm) wide elastic. Fold the hem 1½" (4 cm) to the wrong side and sew a seam ⅛" (2 mm) from the bottom edge. Sew another seam 1⅛" (2.7 cm) up from the first seam. Leave an opening to insert the elastic. Cut a piece of elastic and insert the elastic into casing. Overlap the ends of the elastic and sew them together. Close the opening.

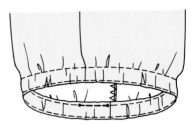

A variation can be obtained by using several rows of ⅜" (1 cm) wide elastic. When sewing the side seam, leave the casing allowance open on one side seam. Fold casing to wrong side and press. Sew the casing seams ½" (1.3 cm) apart.

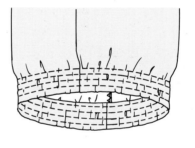
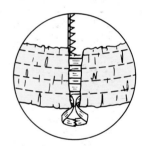

Or you can leave a space between the casing seams, for example, sew ½" (1.3 cm) casings, leaving ¼" (6 mm) spaces between. See illustration. Adjust the allowance for the casing to accommodate as many rows of elastic as you plan to use. Thread the elastic through the open seam on the inside. This finish can also be used on the bottom edge of the sleeves.

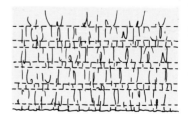

Neckline finish: 7   Design change: F
Hem finish: 6   Patches
Sleeve finish: 6

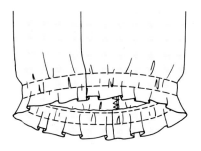

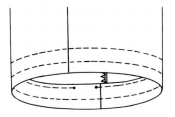

HEM FINISH 7
ELASTIC IN CASING WITH RUFFLED EDGE

This finish can be used on the bottom of the sleeves and/or the bottom of the sweatshirt. Check for correct finished length. Refer to Page 9. Add 2¼" (5.5 cm) hem to the bottom edge, for the casing and the ruffles. Fold the hem to the wrong side and press. From the bottom, measure up 1" (2.5 cm) and sew a seam. Sew another seam 1⅛" (2.7 cm) from the first seam, leaving an opening for inserting the elastic. Cut a piece of 1" (2.5 cm) wide elastic and insert into casing. Overlap the elastic and sew the ends together. Close the opening.

HEM FINISH 8
V-SLIT AT FRONT

When cutting out the sweatshirt, check for correct finished length. Refer to Page 9. Add 3" (7.5 cm) for the hem. Mark the center front at the bottom. Fold the hem to the right side. Mark a V at the center front 2" (5 cm) deep and 1" (2.5 cm) wide at the bottom edge. Sew the V following the marks. Cut out the V ¼" (6 mm) from the stitching line. Clip the seam allowance to the point.

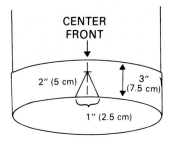
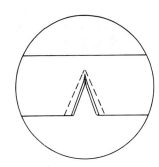

Turn the V inside out and press a 3" (7.5 cm) hem. Sew the hem ¼" (6 mm) from the raw edge. Topstitch ¼" (6 mm) up from the bottom edge all around the bottom of the shirt and around the V.

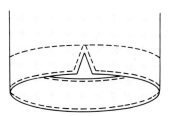

Neckline finish: 5
Hem finish: 8
Sleeve finish: 1

HEM FINISH 9
CURVED HEMLINE WITH RIBBING BINDING

Check for correct finished length. Refer to Page 9. As a variation, you can make a curved hemline, up in the front and down in the back. To do this you have to change the hemline on the pattern. On Master Pattern piece 1 front, at the center front, make a mark approximately 2"-3½" (5 cm-9 cm) up from the bottom edge. Draw a curved line from the mark to the bottom of the side seam. On Master Pattern piece 2 Back, increase the length of the center back the same amount as you shortened the front and draw a curve. To obtain the correct length of binding, measure the entire bottom edge. Cut the binding from ribbing, three quarters of the length of the bottom edge and 3" (7.5 cm) wide.

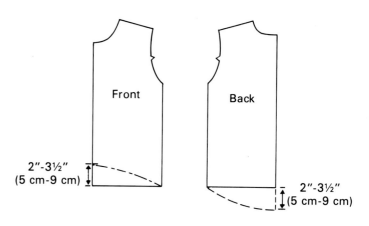

Neckline finish: 9
Hem finish: 9
Sleeve finish: 1

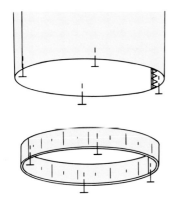

Sew the binding into a circle. Fold the binding double lengthwise, wrong sides together. Divide the binding and the bottom edge of the shirt into fourths with pins.

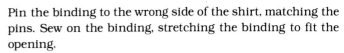

Pin the binding to the wrong side of the shirt, matching the pins. Sew on the binding, stretching the binding to fit the opening.

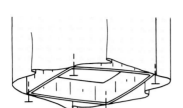

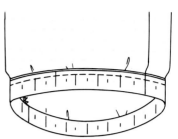

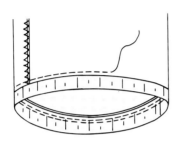

Press the seam allowance toward the shirt. Topstitch through the seam allowance close to the seam. Fold the binding on seam line to the right side and pin in place. Topstitch close to the edge of the binding. This topstitching can be done using a double needle.

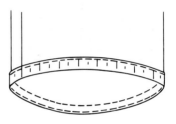

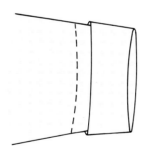

SLEEVE FINISH 10
ROLLED UP SLEEVES WITH CONTRAST FACINGS

A rolled up sleeve made with contrast fabric facing is a very attractive way to finish the sleeves.

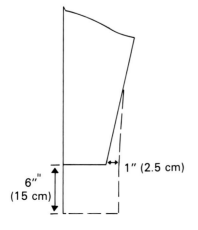

6" (15 cm)

1" (2.5 cm)

At the bottom edge of the sleeve, add to the width 1" (2.5 cm) and mark. Lengthen the sleeve at the bottom edge 6" (15 cm) and draw a line straight through the mark on the sleeve seam. See illustration. Cut out the sleeves; make sure to place sleeve on fold.

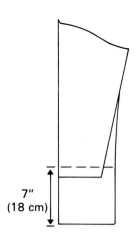

7"
(18 cm)

To make the facing, draw a line 7" (18 cm) up from the bottom edge. Cut out the facing from contrast fabric, be sure to place on fold.

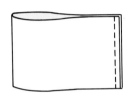

Fold the facing double lengthwise, right side to right side and sew the sleeve seam. Pin the facing to the bottom edge of the sleeve, right side to right side and sew on facing.

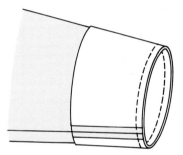

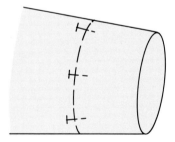

Turn the facing to the inside of the sleeve, sew in place close to the edge of the facing. Turn up the sleeve to form cuff.

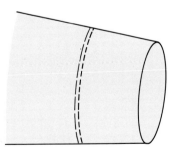

Pockets

What can you do with a pocket? Many things, a pocket can be more than a place for keeping things. Pockets are fun when they are used as decorations and they can be placed almost anywhere. On a sleeve, at the hemline, on the front, at the side. Decorate them with emblems, appliques, topstitching, etc. A pocket can be interesting when you wash the sweatshirt, you may find wrinkled kleenex, soggy notes and even clean money.

POCKET 1
PATCH POCKET

Use Master Pattern piece 14 for a standard shirt pocket. Use Master Pattern piece 15 for a rounded pocket. If you like a square pocket, use Master Pattern piece 15 and make the corners straight. You can use any size pocket on any size shirt.

Fuse interfacing to the wrong side of the pocket facing and overcast the raw edges. Fold the facing on the folding line to the right side and sew each side the width of the facing. If the pocket has rounded corners, continue sewing on the seam line and baste around the curved edges in the middle of the seam allowance.

Turn the facing to the wrong side. Fold under the raw edges and press.

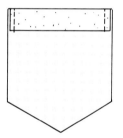 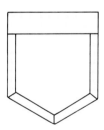

For a rounded pocket, pull on the basting stitches to draw in the seam allowance. Notch out excess seam allowance. Pin the pocket in position on the shirt.

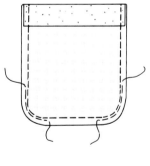 

Topstitch around the pocket, leaving the top open. You can reinforce the top by sewing a small triangle at each corner or sew with a zig-zag stitch ¼" (6 mm) in on each side. When you sew on the pocket, you can topstitch around the pocket with a single or double needle.

Neckline finish: 11
Hem finish: 3

Sleeve finish: 10
Pocket: 1

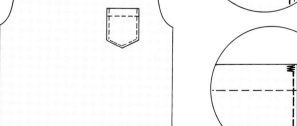

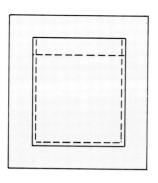

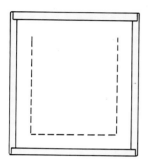

POCKET 2
POCKET ON PATCH
To add interest and color, a pocket can be applied to a patch from a contrasting fabric.

Cut the patch 2" (5 cm) larger than the finished pocket. Place the pocket in the center of the patch and sew the pocket on to the patch. Press under the raw edges of the patch and sew the patch to the shirt.

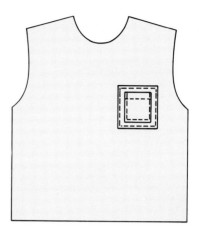

POCKET 3
POCKET WITH CONTRAST BAND
A contrasting band at the top of the pocket made from woven fabric or ribbing is very attractive. You can use pattern piece 14 or 15 for the pocket. When you are cutting out the pocket, cut the pocket ¾" (2 cm) down from the folding line. Cut the band the width of the pocket and 2½" (6.5 cm) high. If You are using ribbing for the band, cut it 1" (2.5 cm) shorter than the pocket so the ribbing can be stretched to fit.

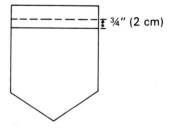

¾" (2 cm)

Fold the band double, wrong side to wrong side and press. Sew the band to the top edge of the pocket, right side to right side. If using ribbing band, stretch band to fit pocket. Fold under the seam allowances of the pocket to the wrong side and press. Sew pocket to shirt.

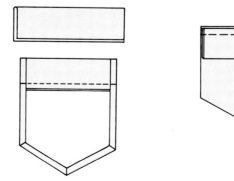

Neckline finish: 14   Sleeve finish: 1
Hem finish: 2   Pocket: 3

46

Neckline finish: 12
Sleeve finish: 1

Sleeve finish: 1
Pocket: 4

POCKET 4
KANGAROO POCKET

Use Master Pattern piece 16. We suggest you interface the pocket facings so they do not stretch. Cut two pieces of fusible interfacing the size of the pocket facing. Fuse the interfacing to facings and overcast the raw edges.

Fold the pocket facings on the folding lines to the wrong side and sew close to the raw edges of the facings. At the sides of the pocket, press the seam allowances to the wrong side.

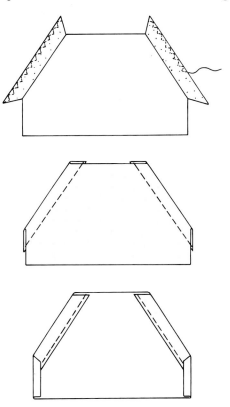

To mark the correct position of the pocket, place the pocket on the front with the right sides up, matching the center front of the pocket to the center front of the shirt. Mark the top edge of the pocket with pins. Mark the pocket placement ½" (1.3 cm) down from the pins.

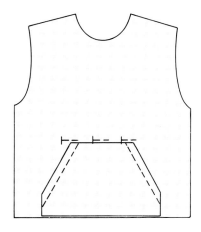

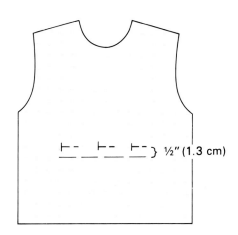

½" (1.3 cm)

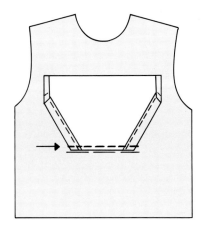

Place the raw edge of the pocket on the placement line, right side to right side. The bottom edge of the pocket is now close to the neckline. Sew the top of the pocket to the shirt. Flip the pocket down and pin it to the bottom edge of the shirt. Topstitch sides of pocket to front and sew the bottom part of the pocket to the shirt.

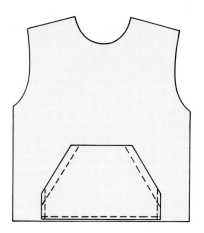

POCKET 5
KANGAROO POCKET WITH PIPING

Use Master Pattern piece 16. Trace the pattern for the pocket, eliminating the facing and add ¼" (6 mm) seam allowance at the facing line.

Cut out the facing, adding ¼" (6 mm) for a seam allowance.

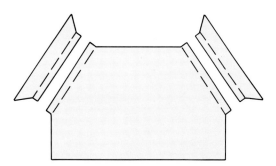

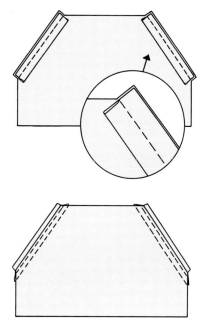

Sew the piping to the pocket along the pocket opening edge. Pin the facing to the pocket over the piping, right sides together, and sew in the same line of stitches.

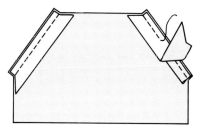

Fold the facing to the wrong side and sew close to the edges of the facing and piping. Sew the pocket on to the shirt using the same procedures as for the kangaroo pocket.

Neckline finish: 1
Hem finish: 1
Sleeve finish: 1
Pocket: 6

POCKET 6
POCKET IN YOKE SEAM

To make the yoke, trace pattern piece for the front. Divide armhole in three and draw a line as shown. To mark the pocket placement, divide the line in half and mark as shown for the center of the pocket.

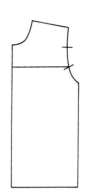 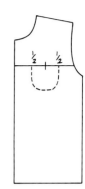

Cut pattern apart and add ⅝" (1.5 cm) seam allowance to the yoke and the front.

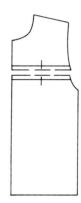

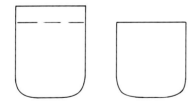

Use Master Pattern piece 15 for the pocket. Trace two pattern pieces, one with facing and one without facing. Mark the pocket opening on the front yoke seam. The pocket opening can be between 4"-5" (10 cm-12.5 cm) depending upon the size of the sweatshirt.

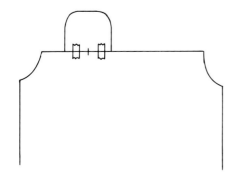

Butt the pocket piece without the facing to the front at pocket placement. Tape in place. Cut out the front, including the pocket.

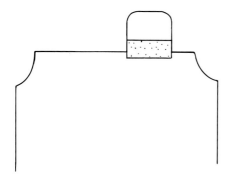

Cut a strip of fusible interfacing approximately 2" (5 cm) wide and fuse to the pocket as illustrated.

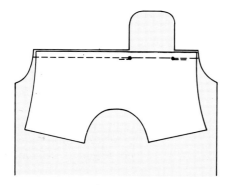

Pin the yoke and the front, right side to right side. Sew the yoke seam using a ⅝" (1.5 cm) seam allowance; when you sew this seam, baste the pocket opening and lock the stitches at the ends of the pocket. See illustration. Press the seam open.

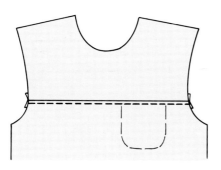

Topstitch ¼" (6 mm) down from the yoke seam. If you wish to have any decorations or a buttonhole on the pocket, this should be done now.

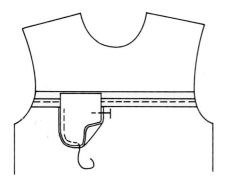

Cut out the pocket with the facing. Pin this piece, right side to right side, to the other pocket piece with the raw edges even. Sew the pocket pieces together.

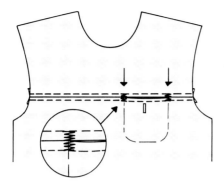

Topstitch ¼" (6 mm) up from yoke seam. On the right side, at the ends of the pocket opening, reinforce the edges of the pocket with a bartack. Remove the basting stitches at the pocket opening.

Neckline finish: 10
Hem finish: 1
Sleeve finish: 1

Design change: F
Pocket: 7

POCKET 7
PATCH POCKET WITH ZIPPER

The zipper on the patch pocket may be placed at the top or at an angle. The size of the pocket will be determined by the length of the zipper. Cut a piece of fabric for the pocket approximately 2" (5 cm) wider than the length of the zipper. Cut another piece of lining or lightweight fabric for the facing, the same width as the pocket and 3" (7.5 cm) long.

On the facing, mark a rectangle the length of the zipper and ¼" (6 mm) wide.

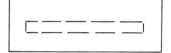

Pin the pocket and the facing, right side to right side. Sew around following the lines.

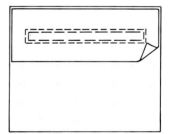

51

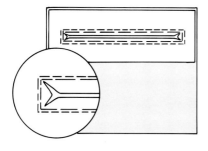

Cut a slit in the middle of the rectangle, stopping ½" (1.3 cm) from either end and clip to each corner. Turn the facing to the wrong side and press, rolling the seam slightly to the facing side.

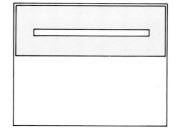

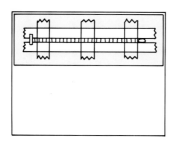

Place the zipper underneath the opening with the zipper teeth exposed. Baste or tape in place.

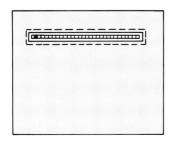

Topstitch around the zipper close to the edge of the fabric.

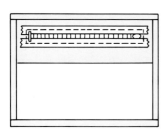

Press the seam allowance around the pocket to the wrong side. Pin the pocket in place. Topstitch all around the pocket.

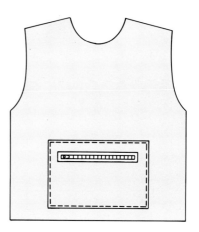

Design Changes

Neckline finish: 6
Hem finish: 6
Sleeve finish: 6

Design change: Basic Patch

The fun part of making a sweatshirt is experimenting with colors and designs. Your possibilities are endless. Create your own design or use the designs in this book. Start with a simple design. After you have made your first design, you will see how easy they are to make. Think of it as a puzzle. The fewer and larger your pieces, the easier your sweatshirt will be to put together.

The designs presented in this book are to give you ideas. The measurements are approximate. You may want to vary the measurements depending upon the size of the sweatshirt.

When you are making your own designs, horizontal and vertical designs are the easiest to make and can be placed at any position of the body of the shirt and on the sleeves.

The first thing you have to do is select neckline, sleeve and hem finish. Trace the pattern pieces.

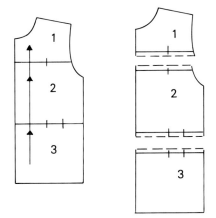

Mark the lines for the design changes on the pattern pieces. Number each piece in the order they will be sewn together. Add grain line to each piece. If you wish, you can make notches; this will make it easier to match the pieces.

Cut the pattern apart and add seam allowances to the new cutting lines. Add ¼" (6 mm) or ⅝" (1.5 cm) if you plan to topstitch the seams. Cut out the pattern pieces. It is a good idea to label each piece with transparent tape so you do not mix them up.

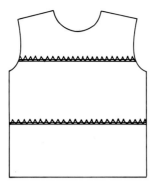

Sew the pieces together and continue sewing shirt; refer to basic instructions and sections for neckline, sleeve and hem finishes you have selected.

Neckline finish: 2
Hem finish: 5
Sleeve finish: 1

Pocket: 1
Design change: A

DESIGN A

Trace two fronts and label left and right front. On the left front, draw a line perpendicular to the center front, at the mark for center of shirt. Cut pattern apart and add seam allowances. Label pieces 1, 2 and 3.

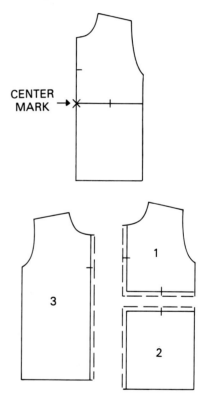

CENTER MARK →

To sew the front, sew 1 to 2 and sew 3 to 1 and 2.

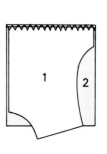

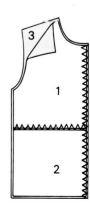

Neckline finish: 2   Sleeve finish: 1
Hem finish: 1   Design change: B

DESIGN B

Measure the pattern from the armhole to the center front and divide this distance into three equal parts. On the mark closest to the center front, draw a line parallel to the center front from the neckline to the bottom edge. Cut pattern piece apart and add seam allowances. Place the center panel on the fold and cut one. Sew the panels together.

This design can be used on both the front and back.

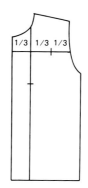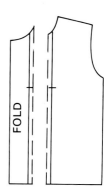

DESIGN C

Divide the shoulder into three equal parts. On the bottom edge, make a mark 1½" (4 cm) to 2½" (6.5 cm) from the center front. Connect the mark closest to the armhole with the mark at the bottom edge. Cut pattern apart and add seam allowances. Place center panel on the fold and cut one. Cut two side panels. Sew the panels together.

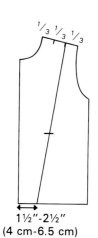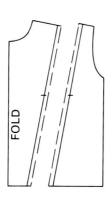

1½"-2½"
(4 cm-6.5 cm)

Neckline finish: 6   Sleeve finish: 1
Hem finish: 4   Design change: C

Neckline finish: 4   Sleeve finish: 1
Hem finish: 1   Design change: D

DESIGN D

Draw a line perpendicular to the center front at the bottom of the armhole. Make a mark on the shoulder ⅜" (1 cm) in from the armhole. Make another mark on the side ½" (1.3 cm) down from the armhole. Draw a diagonal line from the mark on the shoulder to the line at the center front. Draw another diagonal line parallel to the first line from the mark on the side to the center front. Label the pattern pieces 1, 2 and 3.

Cut the pattern pieces apart at the lines and add seam allowances.

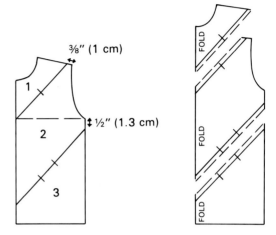

Sew 1 to 2, starting at the shoulder seams down to the point, lower the needle, pivot and sew the other side. Sew 2 to 3 in the same manner.

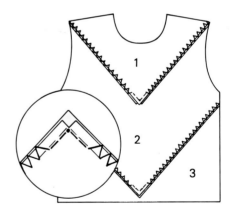

You may want a center front seam. If so, remember to add a seam allowance at the center front. If you are using striped fabric, make sure the stripes will match at the center front when cutting out the pieces.

If you want just a yoke, eliminate the lower cutting line.

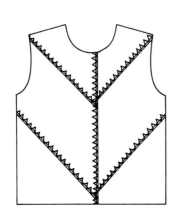

56

DESIGN E

This design for a yoke can be on the front only or both front and back. Draw a line across from the notch at the armhole to the center front. Cut pattern apart and add seam allowance.

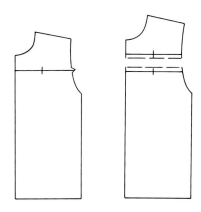

DESIGN F

To make an insert at the shoulder, draw a line on the front pattern piece 2" (5 cm) down from the shoulder. Draw a line ¾" (2 cm) down from the shoulder on the back pattern piece.

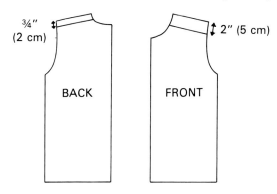

Neckline finish: 1
Hem finish: 1

Sleeve finish: 1
Design change: E

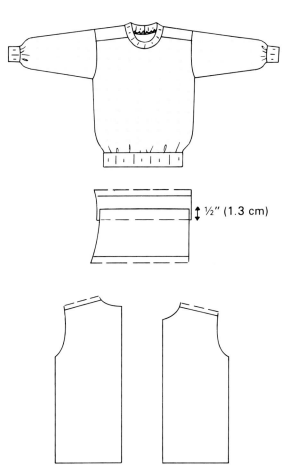

Cut pattern apart on these two shoulder lines. Overlap the two pieces ½" (1.3 cm) matching the armhole and the neckline. Tape the pieces together. Add seam allowances to the insert as well as the back and front. Sew the insert to the front and back.

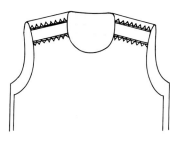

Neckline finish: 2
Hem finish: 1

Sleeve finish: 1
Design change: G

DESIGN G

Draw a line across the front from the notch at the armhole to the center front. Draw another line from the mark for center of shirt to the side seam. Label the pattern pieces 1, 2 and 3. Add notches and cut pattern piece apart on the lines. Add seam allowances.

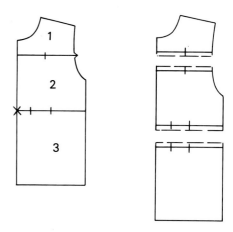

Trace pattern piece 2 twice to obtain a right and left side. Divide pattern piece in half at center front and mark. Draw a bias line through this mark, starting and stopping an equal distance from the center. Cut the pattern piece apart on the bias line. Remember to add seam allowances.

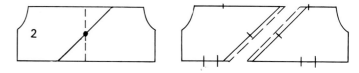

Trace the pattern piece for the sleeve, tracing twice to have a complete sleeve. On the sleeve, draw a line from the notch to the bottom edge of the sleeve, parallel to the center line.

Cut the sleeve apart on this line. Add seam allowances. If using contrasting fabric for the sleeves, be sure to cut one sleeve for the right side and one sleeve for the left side.

Start by sewing the two pieces of 2 together. Sew 1 to 2 and then to 3. Sew the pieces for the sleeve together.

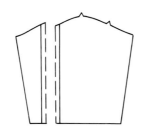

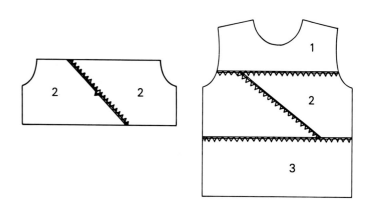

Neckline finish: 5
Hem finish: 1

Sleeve finish: 1
Design change: H

DESIGN H

Trace the complete front. Mark the center front with a broken line. Mark the center of shirt. Draw a line from the notch at the armhole through the mark at the center front, down to the other side. Draw another line, 2" to 3" (5 cm to 7.5 cm) below the first line. On the other side of the front, draw a line from the notch at the armhole to the center mark.

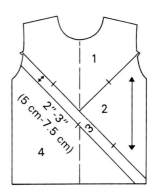

Remember to add grain lines and seam allowances to the pattern pieces. Label the pieces 1, 2, 3 and 4.

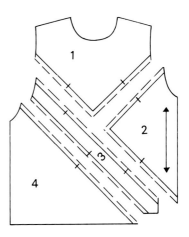

Sew 1 to 2

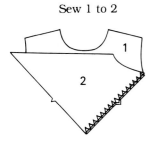

Sew 3 to 1 and 2

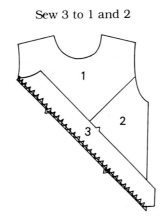

Sew 4 to 3

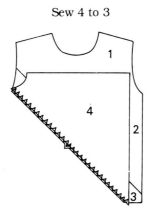

Finished Front

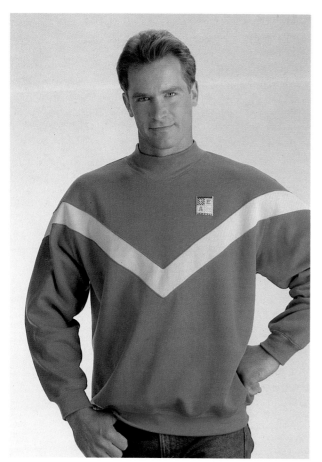

Neckline finish: 7
Hem finish: 1

Sleeve finish: 1
Design change: I

DESIGN I

Trace the pattern pieces for the front and the sleeve. Add ¼" (6 mm) seam allowance to the center of sleeve. Overlap the top part of the sleeve ½" (1.3 cm) over the front armhole. Match the notches on the sleeve and armhole and tape in place.

From the mark for the center of shirt, draw a diagonal line through the notch on the armhole to the edge of the sleeve. Draw another line parallel to this line 2" (5 cm) up from the first line. Label the pattern pieces.

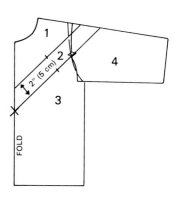

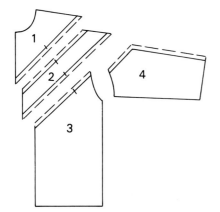

Cut the pattern pieces apart on the lines and add seam allowances. Add seam allowances to the back sleeves at the center sleeve seam and cut out.

Staystitch the points of the V's. Clip to corner of staystitching.

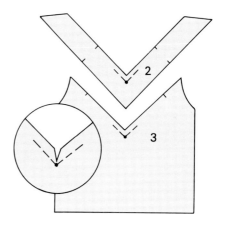

60

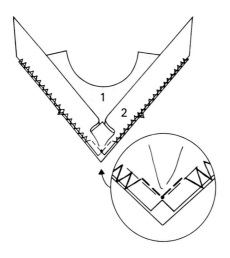

Sew pattern piece 1 to 2, starting at one shoulder seam sew to the point of the V, lower the needle, pivot, and sew the other side.

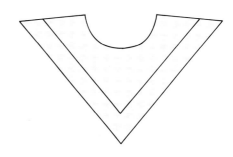

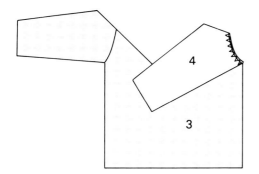

Sew pattern piece 4 to 3 at the armhole.

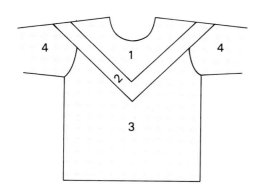

Sew pattern piece 2 to 4 and 3, starting at the shoulder seam, sew to the point of the V, pivot, and sew to the other shoulder seam.

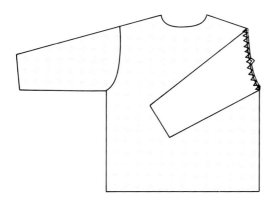

Sew the back sleeve to the back. Sew the shoulder and the center sleeve seams.

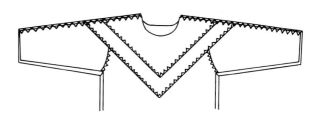

Neckline finish: 3
Hem finish: 1
Sleeve finish: 1

Design change: J
Patch and applique

DESIGN J

This design has an insert at the shoulder down to the bottom of the sleeve. On the front pattern piece draw a line across 2¼" (5.5 cm) down from the shoulder. On the back pattern piece, draw a line ¾" (2 cm) down from the shoulder.

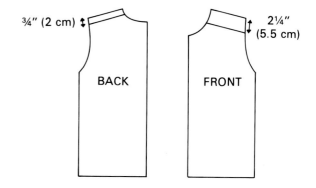

Cut out these two shoulder pieces. Overlap these two pieces ½" (1.3 cm) at the shoulder, matching the armhole and neckline edges and tape the pieces together.

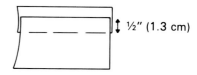

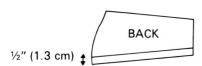

Trace two sleeve pieces and mark them front and back. On the front sleeve piece, draw a parallel line from the top to the bottom of the sleeve 2" (5 cm) from the center of sleeve. On the back sleeve, draw a parallel line ½" (1.3 cm) from the center of sleeve.

Cut the pattern pieces apart at the lines. Butt the two strips together at the center line and tape them in place.

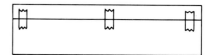

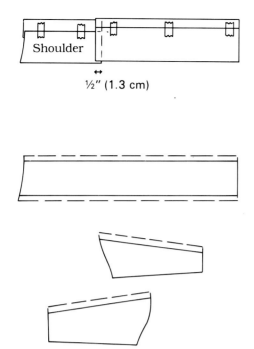

½" (1.3 cm)

Overlap the strip for the sleeve and the strip for the shoulder ½" (1.3 cm) at armhole. Add seam allowances to the strip, sleeve, back shoulder and front shoulder.

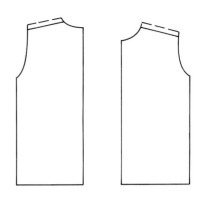

Sew the front sleeve to the front, and the back sleeve to the back.

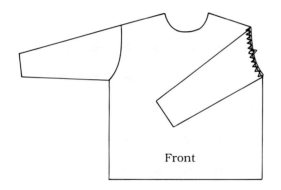

Front

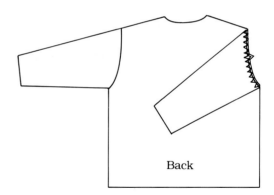

Back

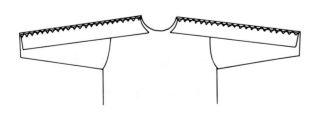

Sew the insert to front and back from the neckline to the bottom of the sleeve.

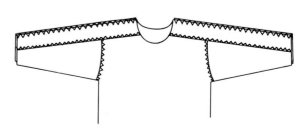

Neckline finish: 2
Hem finish: 1

Sleeve finish: 1
Design change: K

DESIGN K

Trace the front pattern piece. Mark the center of shirt. Make another mark half way between this mark and the bottom edge of the shirt. At each shoulder, make a mark 1" to 2" (2.5 cm to 5 cm) in from the armhole. Draw a line from the mark at the shoulder to the bottom mark at the center front.

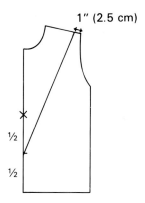

Trace pattern to make complete fronts. On upper front, draw parallel lines 1¾" (4.5 cm) apart as shown. Label the pattern pieces 1 through 6. See illustration. Cut the pattern apart and add the seam allowances.

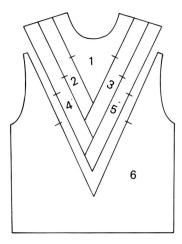

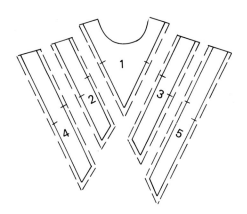

Sew 2 to 1

Sew 3 to 1 and 2

Sew 4 to 2 and 3

Sew 5 to 3 and 4

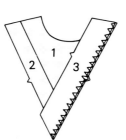

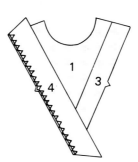

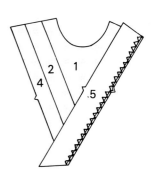

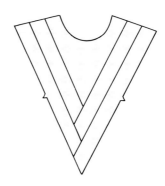

Finished Yoke

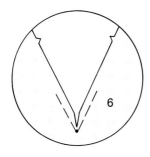

On the front (pattern piece 6) staystitch the point of V. Make a clip down to the stitches at the point of the V.

Sew yoke to front, starting at one shoulder seam, sew down to the point of the V, pivot, and sew the other side.

Decorative Finishes

Neckline finish: 5
Hem finish: 1

Sleeve finish: 1

PATCHES

A patch is basically a piece of fabric sewed to a garment. Patches can be any size or shape. If you are using lightweight fabric or a fabric that ravels, stabilize the fabric with lightweight fusible interfacing.

When you cut out the patch, add ¼" (6 mm) all around the edges. You can add an extra touch to any patch by adding an applique or ribbons. Try combining different size patches to make a border.

If the patch is cut on the bias, we suggest that you staystitch the edges to keep them from stretching. Press the raw edges of the patch to the wrong side. Pin the patch to the sweatshirt and topstitch close to the edges.

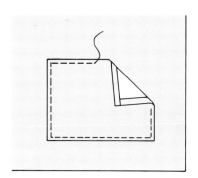

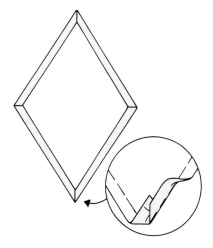

You can also sew on the patch using a satin stitch. In this case, eliminate the seam allowance and make sure to stabilize patch with fusible interfacing. To satin stitch, use a medium or wider zig-zag stitch and a very short stitch length.

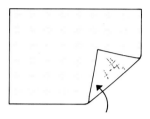

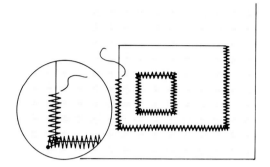

Neckline finish: 1
Hem finish: 1
Sleeve finish: 1

Applique
Border topstitched over
bottom of shirt

APPLIQUES

Appliques can be any shape or size. We have included letters, numbers, crests and diamond shapes. An easy way to make an attractive applique is to use a piece of fabric with a pretty design, such as a flower. Cut out the design and use it for the applique.

We will give basic instructions for applying an applique. For more information, alternate methods, and a great variety of appliques, we recommend the book, "Applique The Kwik•Sew Way".

The easiest way to make an applique is to use paper backed fusible web. Trace the design on the paper side of the fusible web. If using the letters and numbers, trace them to tissue paper first. Turn over the letters and numbers before you trace them to the paper backed fusible web to get a mirror image. Place the rough side of the paper to the wrong side of the fabric for the applique and fuse. Cut out the design and peel off the paper backing.

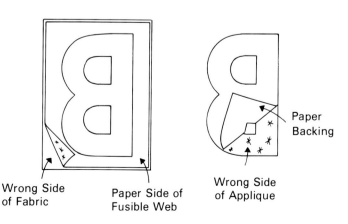

Wrong Side of Fabric

Paper Side of Fusible Web

Wrong Side of Applique

Paper Backing

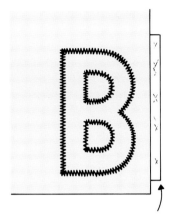

Tear Away Material

Position the applique on the right side of the sweatshirt. Fuse the applique in place. We recommend that you stabilize under the position of the applique with a "tear-away" material.

Sew over the raw edges of the applique using a satin stitch. Tear away the stabilizing material on the wrong side.

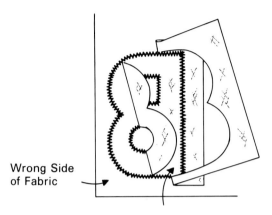

Wrong Side of Fabric

Tear Away Material

CRESTS

Master Pattern piece 23 is for crests in various sizes. The smaller crest can be added to pockets and the larger crests can be placed on the front of the sweatshirt.

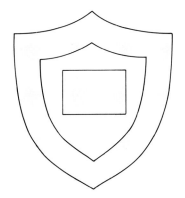

Copy pattern piece for the crest to the paper side of the fusible web. Fuse to the wrong side of the fabric for the crest. Cut out the crest. The crest can be decorated with appliques, letters, ribbons, etc. These should all be added to the crest before it is sewn on to the sweatshirt.

Fuse the crest to the shirt at the desired position and sew around the crest with a satin stitch. If you plan to use buttons, studs, beads, etc., those should be added after you sew on the crest.

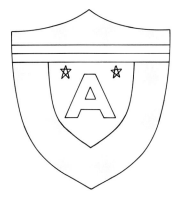  

PADDED OUTLINE DESIGN WITH CUT-OUTS

Outline stitching gives a sweatshirt a very elegant appearance. We have included one design, Master Pattern piece 25. You can design your own, but remember that the areas you plan to cut out should be small and be sure to consider the placement of the cut-outs on your garment. These cut outs can be inside a design, they can be leaves, or the center of a flower.

Transfer the design to a "tear-away" material. If you are using the design around the neckline, it is a good idea to cut the upper part of the shirt from "tear-away" material. Transfer the design, being sure it is even on both sides of the front.

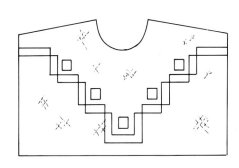

Neckline finish: 1   Sleeve finish: 2
Hem finish: 1   Outline stitching

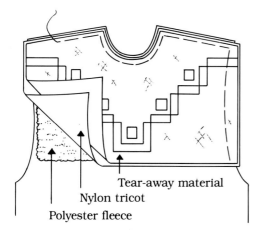

Tear-away material
Nylon tricot
Polyester fleece

Pin polyester fleece to the wrong side of the fabric under the position of the design. Cover the fleece with a lightweight fabric, we recommend using Nylon tricot. Place the "tear-away" material with the transferred design over the tricot and baste to keep in place.

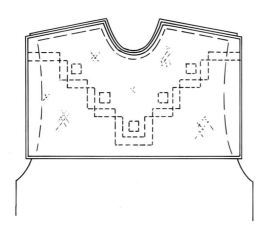

To transfer the design to the right side of the sweatshirt, sew from the wrong side, following all the lines of the design, using a straight stitch.

On the right side, satin stitch over the straight stitches.

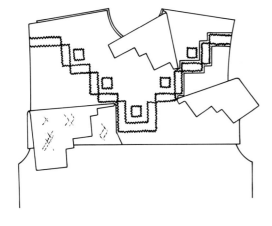

Tear away the stabilizing material on the wrong side.

On the wrong side, cut the tricot and the fleece close to the stitches; leave the fleece and the tricot in the areas you wish to have padded.

On the right side, very carefully, cut out the squares.

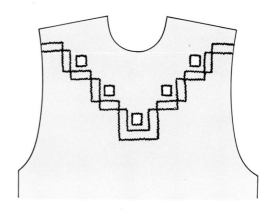

Neckline finish: 1
Hem finish: 1

Sleeve finish: 1
Ribbon trim

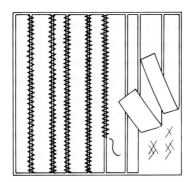

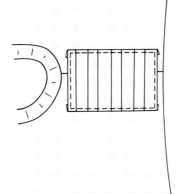

RIBBON TRIM

You can use ribbons in all sizes and colors to give a sweatshirt a special touch. When you work with ribbons, we recommend that you pre-wash the ribbons to make sure they do not shrink when you wash the sweatshirt.

If using ribbon ¼" (6 mm) wide or wider, it is best to fuse the ribbon to the sweatshirt before you sew it on, using strips of fusible web ⅛" (3 mm) wide. This will prevent the ribbon from puckering.

When you sew on a ribbon which is ¼" (6 mm) wide or wider, sew on both edges of the ribbon. A narrow ribbon should be sewed in the middle.

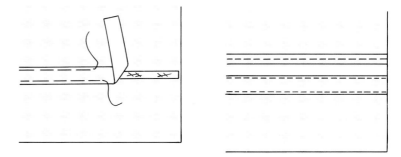

An easy way to apply ribbon when you have more than one strip, is to use lightweight fusible interfacing. If you wish to trim the shoulders with ribbons which are stitched together, decide the size desired; approximately 4" to 5" (10 cm to 13 cm) wide and the length of the shoulder. Cut fusible interfacing twice this width, this will accommodate both shoulders. Place the ribbons on the fusible side of the interfacing, butting the edges together and fuse. Sew the strips together, using a narrow zig-zag stitch. Be sure to catch both edges of the ribbon with your stitches. Cut the piece in half.

When you sew the ribbons to the sweatshirt, fold under the raw edges and sew all around the ribbons.

You can make a decorative design from ribbons. Cut ribbons 3¾" (9.5 cm), 3¼" (8 cm) and 2¾" (7 cm) long. Fold under ends of each piece of ribbon ¼" (6 mm) and press. Pin to shirt as shown and stitch close to all edges. Add a small purchased applique below the ribbons, see illustration.

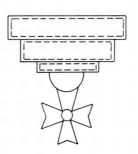

Neckline finish: 1   Sleeve finish: 1
Hem finish: 1   Country yoke

DECORATIVE YOKES

Decorative yokes can be made from any contrast woven fabric, you can use a solid, print or striped fabric. These yokes are placed on top of the sweatshirt and topstitched. Be sure to cut out the complete front.

COUNTRY LOOK YOKE

For a country look, use calico prints and eyelet trim. You can use two prints and alternate the fabrics or you can make each strip a different color or print.

To make pattern piece for yoke, use front Master Pattern piece 1, make a mark 1⅝" (4 cm) up from the mark for the center of the shirt. Mark 1⅝" (4 cm) up from notch on armhole. Draw a line from mark to mark. Copy the yoke pattern piece and add ¼" (6 mm) seam allowances at the center front and to the bottom edge. When cutting out the shirt, be sure to cut out the complete front. The yoke will be placed on top of the sweatshirt.

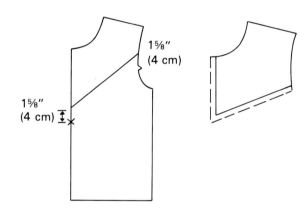

To stabilize the yoke, cut a piece of lightweight woven fabric approximately 12" x 36" (30 cm x 92 cm). Plan the order and the color of the strips. Cut strips of fabric on the bias 1½" (4 cm) wide and approximately 36" (92 cm) long.

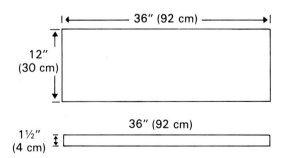

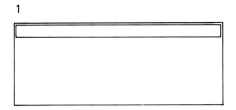

1

Place one strip even with the long edge of the stabilizing fabric with the right side up. Place the next strip on top of the first strip, right sides together and sew through both pieces and the stabilizing fabric, using a ¼" (6 mm) seam allowance. Flip the top piece over and sew on the third strip using the same procedure. Continue until you have covered the entire stabilizing fabric.

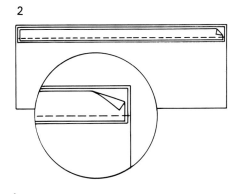

2

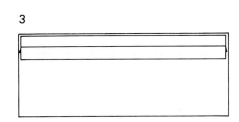

3

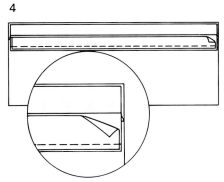

4

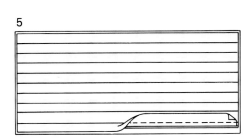

5

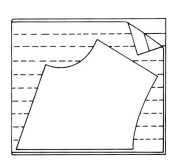

Fold the fabric in half, right sides together, matching the seams. Place yoke on fabric with bottom edge even with the first strip. Cut out the yokes.

Use pre-gathered eyelet or lace to trim yoke. Place lace or eyelet to bottom edge of each yoke, right sides together, and stitch. Remove the binding on the eyelet or lace to reduce bulk. Press seam allowance toward yoke. Repeat for other yoke.

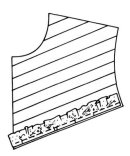
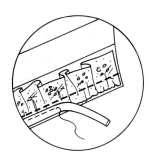
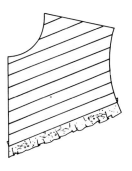

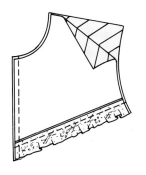

Pin center front seam, right sides together, matching seams and stitch from neckline to bottom edge of lace.

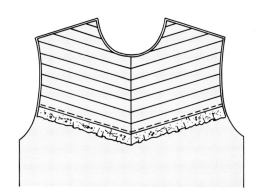

Pin the yoke to the front with the right side up, matching the neckline and armhole edges. Topstitch close to the bottom edge of the yoke.

If you wish, you can cut away the shirt fabric under the yoke. If you leave the fabric, sew close to the edges of the neckline and armholes to keep it in place.

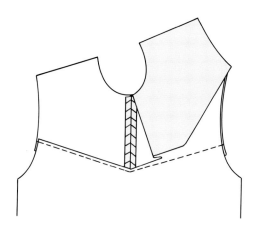

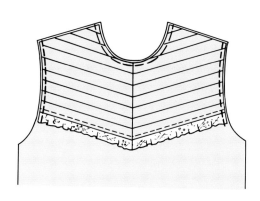

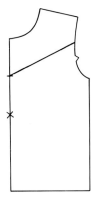

YOKE FROM SHEER FABRIC

This yoke can be made from organza, handkerchief linen, crinkled cotton, or gauze. The sweatshirt is cut away under the yoke after the yoke is stitched to garment; yoke will be transparent.

To make yoke, use front Master Pattern piece 1. On front, divide the distance from mark for center of shirt to neckline in half. Draw a line from armhole to mark. Copy yoke pattern. Cut out yoke from the sheer fabric, placing center front on fold. If using very lightweight and/or sheer fabric, you may wish to use two layers of the fabric.

Neckline finish: 9
Hem finish: 1

Sleeve finish: 1
Yoke

Fold under the bottom raw edge of the yoke ¼" (6 mm) to the wrong side and press.

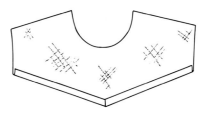

Pin yoke to shirt with right sides up, matching neckline and armhole edges and sew close to the bottom edge of the yoke. Trim away the sweatshirt fabric under the yoke.

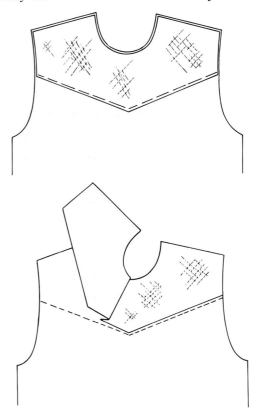

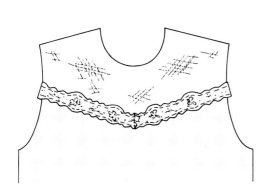

If desired, you can cover the seam with lace. Cut lace the length of the outside edge of the yoke, allowing extra length for matching. Fold the lace in half, matching the design and mark center front with a pin.

Center the lace over the seam, matching pin to center front. Miter the lace if necessary at center front. Pin in place. Stitch along both edges of the lace.

Neckline finish: 1
Hem finish: 1
Sleeve finish: 1

Lace yoke
Ribbon bows

LACE YOKE

You can make an attractive yoke using lace. Use instructions for cutting yoke on Page 72 or design your own. When you cut out the yoke, place the center front on the fold.

The outside edge of the yoke is finished with narrow lace. Place the narrow lace on the lace yoke with right sides up and the scalloped edge of the lace along the raw edge of the yoke. Fold the lace at the center front to miter the corner. Baste close to the inner edge of the lace. Trim the lace yoke under the narrow lace, close to the stitches.

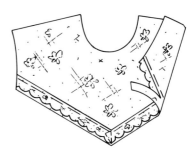

Pin the yoke to the front, matching the center front, neckline and armhole edges. Sew close to the neckline and armhole edges to keep in place. Topstitch close to the inner edge of the lace. Remove basting stitches.

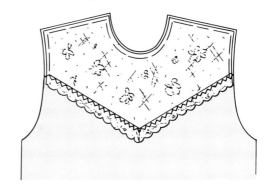

This procedure can be used to cover any part of the garment with lace or contrast fabric. Cover the raw edges with ribbon instead of narrow lace. For example, at the lower edge of front or below the armhole.

BOWS

It is fun to decorate with bows. Place them at shoulders, scatter them over the front, or form a row on one side.

Bows can be from one color or coordinated colors and they can be any size. We will give instructions for a 1½" x 4" (4 cm x 10 cm) bow.

For each bow, cut a piece of fabric 8" x 3½" (20 cm x 9 cm). Fold in half, right sides together and sew the long edge. Press seam open. Turn right side out and press with the seam in the middle.

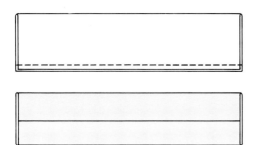

Neckline finish: 7
Hem finish: 6
Sleeve finish: 1

Length added to make dress length
Bows

Fold the bow as shown and sew across the center to secure the ends. Wrap a piece of fabric around the center of the bow and secure with hand stitches. Attach bows to shirt with hand stitches.

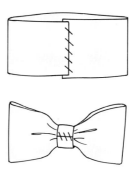

BOW IN GATHERED CASING

Finish shirt with a hem. Mark the position of the casing, approximately half way between the center front and the side seam and 10" (25.5 cm) long. Make two vertical buttonholes ½" (1.3 cm) apart.

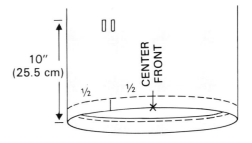

Cut a strip of fabric 11" (28 cm) long and 2" (5 cm) wide. Overcast all of the edges.

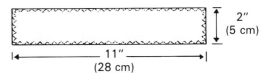

Pin the casing to the wrong side of the shirt over the buttonholes. Fold under the bottom of the strip ¼" (6 mm). Sew close to the long edges and the top edge. Sew in the middle of the strip to form casings.

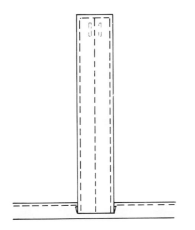

Neckline finish: 9
Hem finish: 2

Sleeve finish: 1

For the tie, cut a piece of fabric 40" x 2" (101 cm x 5 cm). Fold the strip in half, right sides together, and stitch, leaving an opening for turning. Turn right side out and close opening.

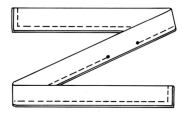

Insert tie through the buttonholes as shown and tie into a bow. If desired, you can use a ribbon for the tie instead of the fabric.

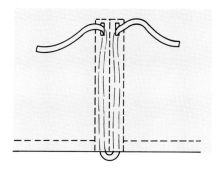

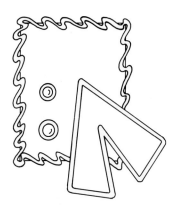

PAINTING

It is really fun to decorate your sweatshirt with paints. You don't have to be an artist, you can get ideas from magazines, pictures, coloring books or you can just have fun with lines, squiggles, dots and splashes. You will be amazed how much it will add to your patches and appliques. You can even apply patches and appliques with paints, no sewing, really Kwik and Easy.

Fabric paints come in jars or bottles. Some have applicator tips and can be applied right out of the bottle or with a brush, others are applied with brush or sponge. A stiff bristle brush size 10 works well and a small fine brush is used for small detail areas.

Do all the painting before the shirt is sewn together, it will be a lot easier. Place a piece of wax paper or aluminum foil under the area to be painted. Secure the painting area with tape or pin to a cutting board to keep the garment from shifting.

Neckline finish: 2
Hem finish: 1
Sleeve finish: 1
Painting

Try some of these ideas:
Paint using various size brushes. Apply a strip of ribbon or sequins in the middle of the stroke and sew on with hand or machine stitches.

Fuse applique or patch to garment and paint around the raw edges to keep the applique in place.

Add shading to the applique with brush strokes.

Paint any detail area on the applique or patch.

Make a template from heavy paper in any shape desired and paint with brush or sponge.

Paint a number, letter, names or dots.

Make brush strokes and add squiggly lines.

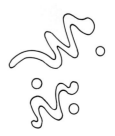